HOA HELL

California Homeowners' Definitive Guide to Beating Bad HOAs

Michael B. Kushner, Esq.

ISBN 979-8-9932696-1-0 (Hardcover)

ISBN 979-8-9932696-2-7 (Paperback)

ISBN 979-8-9932696-0-3 (Ebook)

This book is dedicated to my son, Logan.

He is my most enduring inspiration and motivation.

And, to one of my main motivators,
without whom I would've taken another year or two before writing
this book, and a lover of complex cryptograms:

!KlIEj;::A&/gP$Q7^1&qeYPXH-;Vg2U6?7_ps3`T-)SA\;haIl/
PTHI%Qo&e]UUe9<imS?ZquI5o]`bn%]6A(X]fq$Q-)
oJLEt@*=H$+,_gbDie&2Mam*>dG7q(4?3qH5%`[ig!pU;k20*1S"r\
NO4]@X\PvoeUu;@V^<$*rA3/4Wf$0D+hq.!J6d@2Z2<;1Y;T4o\p]
J=Yk%g]c%[!%Yk/6p&!eRm0kM8q]Kq7X4fY>2F^a!X@<<]
cCk`(W[0%8*U5Bo5V&bD)/k>+"k1:7"t7e_B>^c>9jF*6&?hG_
qcV>UeGgd2#rVfH7=U3PS$@PoBmV-2#4DRVS5o@rE2^G9q9D9Y-
F@o"3qHqM2WfXcY+XbG[?4VQ`Pq>qY]7Bc6XZlX

A heartfelt thank you.

Legal Disclaimer

This publication, HOA HELL | California Homeowners' Definitive Guide to Beating Bad HOAs, is published for educational and informational purposes only. It is intended to provide a broad overview of issues that commonly arise in disputes involving homeowners associations under California law. Nothing in this book should be interpreted as individualized legal advice, nor does reading it create an attorney-client relationship with the author, his law firm, or the publisher.

Laws change, and their application often depends on specific facts and circumstances. Because every homeowner's situation is unique, you should not rely on the material presented here when making any decisions about your particular situation, legal rights, or obligations. If you require legal advice about your particular matter, you should consult with a licensed attorney who can evaluate your case directly. The author and publisher expressly disclaim any liability for actions taken or not taken based on the contents of this book.

Any references to people, boards, or situations in this book are provided for illustrative purposes only. Unless specifically identified as a real case or statute, they should be understood as generalized examples. Unless explicitly stated otherwise, any resemblance to actual persons, communities, or disputes is purely coincidental.

By reading this book, you acknowledge that it is a general resource only and agree not to hold the author or publisher responsible for any outcomes, losses, or damages connected to its use.

Contents

INTRODUCTION

The Birth of a Pioneer

I DIDN'T SET out to become a pioneer in homeowner-side HOA law. In fact, when I first launched my own firm in 2005, then called The Kushner Law Firm, my focus was business and real estate litigation. I handled trials. I negotiated deals. I litigated business and corporate disputes, and I litigated real estate-related disputes, including those involving HOA members. But as a niche? HOA law wasn't yet on my radar. I wasn't aware of anyone else on the homeowner-side claiming mastery of that niche area of the law, so it didn't yet occur to me to do that.

In 2010, I started seeing a lot of cases come in from homeowners who were in terrible disputes with their HOAs. And it wasn't just one or two rogue boards we were seeing. This was systemic. Now, my firm had a good deal of experience with HOA law already. We'd litigated numerous such cases before, and always on the homeowner-side. But we started seeing a lot more. Something had changed. At the same time, I noticed something else: I couldn't find a single law firm that focused exclusively on representing homeowners in HOA disputes.

I remember this one client who came to me after her HOA accused her of running an illegal business out of her home. Apparently, she tutored a few of the kids in the neighborhood once a week at her dining room table. Keep in mind that these were the kids of fellow residents of the association, so there were no cars, no signs, no disturbances. No increased traffic or use of amenities at all. Just a few middle school students quietly getting help with homework. The board nonetheless demanded that she cease all activity immediately or face daily fines and legal action. Meanwhile, another homeowner, who happened to be a sitting board member, was actually operating a full-time massage studio out of his garage, complete with advertisements and numerous customers per day driving through the community. The board never said a word about that.

But the story that still stays with me is this: two of my clients—an elderly couple, ages 98 and 99—were both in end-of-life hospice care at home, confined to their beds in an Orange County 55+ community. They spent their final days doing the only thing that they could still do. They listened to classic musicals like Showboat and Oklahoma on cable channels dedicated to airing such programs. Their son, who was also their full-time caretaker, kept the TV on low throughout the day and night to soothe them. In the middle of an unrelated dispute, where the HOA accused them, without evidence, of creating an unsanitary condition that resulted in a vermin infestation, the board held a hearing that neither of them could attend (because neither of them was even fully conscious). And afterward, the HOA cut off their cable TV. Their only comfort. Their only connection to joy. Just gone.

That wasn't just overreach. That was cruelty. And it made me very angry.

And that's when it clicked. If this was happening in HOA-after-HOA, and I couldn't find a quality law firm that had made it their mission to take this on, maybe I could do a lot more than just win individual cases. Maybe I could build the kind of legal framework homeowners had never had before. Maybe I could focus my attention on fighting for people who actually deserved to win. That's when I started building what would eventually become the first[1] full-scale legal strategy and litigation model on the homeowner side of California HOA law.

---

1. At least that I know of.

Building the System that Changed Everything

What started as case-by-case problem solving quickly evolved into something more strategic. Most law firms that handled these types of cases handled them like one-off disputes. But I began to see patterns: where the breakdowns happened, what boards ignored, what scared typical real estate attorneys, and how to build leverage before filing a single legal document.

That's when I started building methods and systems.

I created internal protocols for how to handle document requests under Civil Code section 5200. I developed sophisticated Internal Dispute Resolution and Alternative Dispute Resolution workflows that escalated pressure on boards without escalating costs for the client. I built color-coded templates for demand letters, statutory notices, and follow-up correspondence that allowed me to move quickly while still tailoring each response. I drafted detailed instructions on "pain points" and internal memos for my staff to follow at every stage of a dispute, so that every client, regardless of matter size, would receive a consistent, strategic, and aggressive response.

The methods and systems that I created became the foundation for how we would handle every HOA case going forward. Those systems worked. They helped me secure favorable results for clients across California. But they also did something else: they turned what had once been a fragmented and overlooked corner of real estate law into a focused, repeatable legal discipline honed to help homeowners force their HOAs to comply with the law.

As my templates became more advanced, I began developing proprietary software to manage, populate, and track them across the firm. That software evolved into a sophisticated legal toolset—custom-built to support the systems I had created. We used it to streamline workflows, reduce client costs, and ensure nothing fell through the cracks. I still use that software today.

In fact, today, my firm's largest competitors on the homeowner-side of HOA law in California use some or all of my methods and systems that they learned while they were employed by me.

By 2019, the systems that I had created were running at full scale. My staff knew how to execute every phase of the homeowner-side playbook. Our internal workflows ensured that no client ever walked into an IDR session unprepared, no board ever got a free pass for violating Civil Code deadlines, and no HOA attorney ever received an ADR demand letter that wasn't part of a larger, pressure-tested sequence.

The Law That Governs Everything

If you've never heard of the Davis-Stirling Common Interest Development Act (Civil Code §§ 4000–6150) (the "Davis-Stirling Act"), don't feel bad because you're not alone. But this body of law controls nearly every aspect of life in a California homeowners association, more commonly referred to as an "HOA." The Davis-Stirling Act spells out what powers HOA boards have, what procedures they must follow, and what rights homeowners can assert when things go wrong. It covers everything from elections and rule enforcement, to budgets, maintenance, records, and disputes.

I wrote this book to help you demystify the Davis-Stirling Act, and to learn to understand and use those laws to protect your rights and increase your enjoyment of your property. Throughout the chapters that follow, you'll see references to the Davis-Stirling Act as the central framework. When other laws apply, like the Corporations Code or the Government Code, I'll point those out. But make no mistake: the Davis-Stirling Act is the starting point and the battleground for nearly every fight between homeowners and HOA boards in California.

Why this Book Exists

If you live in a California HOA and feel like the deck is stacked against you, you're right.

You're told it's a "democracy." That the board represents you. That if you don't like the rules, you can vote, run for office, or speak up at a meeting. But if you've ever actually tried to do those things, you've probably already discovered the truth: in most HOAs, power isn't shared, it's hoarded.

What happens when you speak up? You get ignored. Or fined. Or singled out. You're branded a troublemaker. Maybe you get letters from the HOA's lawyer. Maybe they start enforcing rules differently—i.e., just for you.

And if you push harder by demanding answers, organizing neighbors, or requesting documents, you quickly learn just how far the board, management, and even their attorneys will go to shut you down.

This book is for homeowners who are tired of being intimidated, dismissed, or lied to. It's for people who want to fight back without risking their reputations. And it's for people who've realized that "self-governance" in an HOA doesn't mean much when the people doing the governing answer to no one.

Many homeowners who pick up this book will already have stories of their own. Maybe you were threatened with fines for something your neighbor got away with. Maybe you were ignored when you asked for records. Or maybe you've been hit with a sudden special assessment that seemed to come out of nowhere. Those experiences are not just "frustrations." They are signs of boards violating the law—and they are exactly why this book exists.

The Davis-Stirling Act is not a mystery novel written in code. It is an organized set of statutes. And once you learn its key provisions, you'll see that most of what abusive boards get away with depends on homeowners not knowing those rules. That's why knowledge here is power. Because the moment you understand what the law actually requires, you can stop taking the board's word for it and start insisting on compliance with the law.

And make no mistake, this isn't about theory or abstract analysis. It's about real-world battles, real statutory protections, and real tactics that work. The stories and strategies here are drawn from real-world disputes where homeowners just like you beat the most entrenched and hellish boards at their own game.

Why I Wrote this Book (and Why It's Not Like Any Others)

There are other books about HOAs. But most of them are either written by people who lack actual practical experience in HOA law, or worse, by lawyers who represent HOAs. I noticed that some of those other books, including some purporting to be on the homeowner-side, were heavy on marketing polish and catchy slogans, but light on actual legal guidance. They read like law firm brochures dressed up as battle plans—full of dramatics, but empty on real tools, enforceable rights, or practical solutions for California homeowners.

This book is different.

This book pulls back the curtain.

You'll learn the real legal tools California law gives you, and you'll learn how to use them.

You'll learn what your HOA can't legally do (even though they try).

You'll learn how to protect your rights without falling into the traps most boards, and most HOA-side lawyers, set for unsuspecting home-owners.

And you'll see why the "rules" are often not the problem. It's the people who abuse them.

What You're Up Against

HOA boards don't operate like public agencies. There's no neutral oversight. No ombudsman. No state watchdog agency ready to jump on board violations.

You can't "report" your board to Sacramento. The Department of Real Estate won't touch it. The Attorney General won't investigate. And the Office of the Ombudsperson that once existed for HOAs in California was quietly eliminated years ago.

That means the people who control your community, i.e., the ones who can impose fines, restrict access, control the budget, and even lien your home, often answer to no one.

Unless you make them.

This book will show you how to do exactly that.

Who This Book is For

If your board refuses to respond to your complaints, ignores maintenance problems, enforces rules selectively, ignores their fiduciary duties, or uses the disciplinary process to intimidate you, you're in the right place.

If you've been accused of "harassment" for showing up to meetings or asking tough questions, this book will explain how to push back.

If you've received a cease-and-desist letter from the HOA's attorney, or threats of a hearing, or demands for reimbursement of legal fees, we'll walk you through what's real, what's posturing, and what to do next.

If your HOA is falling apart, physically, financially, or ethically, and the board refuses to act, you'll learn how to force action through Civil Code-backed demands, legal notice, document requests, and (when necessary) recall efforts, internal dispute resolution, or formal legal action.

And if you haven't experienced any of that yet? Read this book now so that you'll be prepared if and when the time comes.

How this Book Works

This book is divided into four parts, each one building on the last.

- **Part I: The System Is Rigged (But You Can Still Win).** Why HOAs get away with abuse, what powers boards actually have under the Davis-Stirling Act, and how the structure stacks the deck (and exactly what that means for you).

- **Part II: Your Legal Rights (And How to Use Them).** This is the heart of the book because it's where I provide you with my core toolkit: records and transparency, annual disclosures/reserves, discipline and due process (including the 2025 AB 130 changes), assessments/maintenance, and architectural control. Plain-English explanations with statute cites and practical steps.

- **Part III: Taking Back Control (Elections, Recalls, IDR/ADR, and When to Litigate).** How to force engagement through IDR/ADR, run fair elections and recalls (including 2025 e-balloting rules), and decide when court is the right move. I also discuss what enforcement and fee-shifting actually look like.

- **Part IV: The Homeowner Playbook: Stacking Your Rights to Assert Maximum Leverage.** A step-by-step strategy to connect the dots: sequence records demands with disclosure failures, pair due-process defects with selective-enforcement proof, time actions around elections, and use ADR or litigation to turn private abuse into public accountability. When you finish the book, you'll be armed with what you need to know and ready to act.

Taken together, these parts form a playbook for surviving and defeating abusive HOAs. You'll see how the law really works, where the traps are hidden, and how to turn each right into leverage. You don't need to master everything at once. Start with the section that speaks to your problem, use the tools there, and build from there. By the time you finish, you won't just understand what your HOA can and can't do, you'll know how to fight back and win.

What You WON'T Find in this Book.

You won't find legal fluff. No abstract theory. No "it depends" analysis that leaves you guessing. And no checklists written by lawyers who've never actually represented a homeowner in court.

Everything in this book is grounded in the actual statutes that govern California HOAs, specifically, the Davis-Stirling Act. We'll cite the relevant Civil Code sections, explain what they mean in plain English, and show you how to use them to your advantage.

We won't quote case law. But we will tell you what the courts have actually done and what they'll expect from you when your rights are on the line.

You'll also find sample strategies, attorney tips, attorney Q&As, document requests, and demand letter language that should prove very helpful to you.

This book doesn't ask for your admiration or exist to glorify myself or my law firm. It exists to give you specific information and tools that work.

And if your HOA doesn't like that—and they won't—too bad.

1

WHAT EVERY CALIFORNIA HOMEOWNER NEEDS TO KNOW ABOUT HOAs

F OR MOST PEOPLE, buying a new home is an achievement, and rightly so. But since more and more residential communities are governed by HOAs in California, it's important for homeowners living in those associations to understand that in addition to buying a new home, they're also buying into a private form of government—a legal structure with rules, penalties, and enforcement powers that often mimic the powers of local government. These private governments are known as homeowners associations, or HOAs, and they govern millions of properties in California.

The Davis-Stirling Act is the primary body of law that governs HOAs in California. It gives boards significant authority to carry out their duties, the most important of which are to maintain the common areas, enforce the governing documents, and collect assessments in an amount sufficient to operate the HOA in compliance with applicable laws. But it also imposes strict requirements on how that power must be exercised, and homeowners who understand those requirements are in a much better position to push back when boards overreach.

This chapter sets the foundation for everything that follows. It explains what HOAs are, how they're structured, what legal documents control them, their powers and limitations, and what obligations they owe to homeowners. If you've ever felt like your board is making up the rules as it goes, this chapter will show you exactly what the law allows and what it doesn't.

The Biggest Mistake Most Homeowners Make

If you live in a community governed by a homeowners association in California, you probably signed more than 100 pages of legally binding documents when you bought your home. You likely received a package containing some CC&Rs, a set of HOA rules, bylaws, architectural guidelines, and multiple disclosure forms. And you probably didn't read most of them.

That's not your fault. You were never expected to.

Documents like these are treated like boilerplate. Buyers don't review the fine print, and no one expects them to—not the realtors, not the lenders, not even the boards themselves. The documents get signed, scanned, and forgotten.

But the minute escrow closes, everything changes. You're now legally subject to all of those governing documents (e.g., the CC&Rs, Articles, Bylaws, Rules, etc.).

Suddenly, the HOA starts citing those same documents as justification for whatever the board wants to do, whether it's denying a request, threatening a hearing, or sending an aggressive letter from their lawyer.

And because most homeowners never read those documents, and have no way of knowing what their rights are under California law, they assume that the board must be right...that whatever the HOA says is enforceable. That the board gets the final word.

That's the biggest mistake homeowners make.

Because the truth is your HOA only has the powers California law and your governing documents explicitly give it. Nothing more.

And if *you* don't know what those limitations are, your board will never tell you.

Where Your HOA's Power Comes From

Most homeowners never think about how their HOA was created. They just assume that it "came with the house." But HOAs aren't natural. They're manufactured constructs that serve a particular purpose. And the people who created them weren't public officials or consumer advocates. They were land developers.

In the 1970s and 80s, California developers started building large communities with shared amenities—parks, pools, clubhouses, greenbelts—and they needed a way to maintain all of it without sticking around. So, they created associations. They drafted governing documents, assigned basic legal powers to a board, and handed over control to the homeowners once a certain number of units sold.

That's how most HOAs are born. And today, there are over 50,000 HOAs (with over 14 million people living within those HOAs) in California.

Most of those HOAs in California are set up as nonprofit mutual benefit corporations. Some are just unincorporated associations. But regardless of how they're structured, once they're up and running, they all derive their power from two places:

1. **The governing documents**—like CC&Rs, Bylaws, and Rules—that act like a contract between the homeowners and the association.

2. **California's Davis-Stirling Act**—a set of laws that spell out what HOA boards can and can't legally do.

When a board acts within those boundaries, its power is real. But when it steps outside them, and far too many do, it creates real problems.

The problem is that most homeowners don't know where the lines are, and their boards are counting on that. That's why it's so important to understand exactly which documents and laws control your HOA and which ones take priority when there's a conflict.

Understanding the Hierarchy of Governing Documents

Every HOA is controlled by a variety of documents, but those documents don't all carry the same weight. There is a strict legal hierarchy, or order, to those documents that establishes which one controls if there's ever a direct conflict between them. Knowing that order puts you in a much stronger position when the board tries to enforce something questionable.

Here's the order to your HOA's governing documents:

- **CC&Rs (Covenants, Conditions, and Restrictions)**. The most important and senior of the governing documents for your community. CC&Rs are recorded with the county and binding on all current and future owners, and they supersede all other governing documents.

- **Articles of Incorporation**. The HOA's formation document, filed with the California Secretary of State. In the vast majority of HOAs, the Articles of Incorporation will have little, if any, bearing on any issues related to homeowner rights or powers.

- **Bylaws**. The operating manual for how your HOA is run, including meetings, elections, and the basic powers of the board.

- **Operating Rules, Regulations, and Architectural Guidelines**. The lowest tier of authority. These can only fill in the details without contradicting any of the superior documents listed above. If they do, they're unenforceable.

And sitting on top of the governing documents you'll find federal, state, and local laws (in that order). In other words, federal, state (e.g., the Davis-Stirling Act), and local law will trump the governing documents, including the CC&Rs, in any direct conflict. There are hundreds of examples of this, but one in particular is Civil Code section 4740, which prohibits HOAs from enforcing new short-term rental restrictions on homeowners who owned their properties prior to the implementation of the new rule.

Why does all this matter? Because if the board enforces something that conflicts with a higher-ranking authority in this list, the higher one controls, no matter how confident the board sounds. That's why it's worth reading your CC&Rs from start to finish at least once. They are the foundation for almost every dispute you'll ever have with your HOA, and understanding them makes it much harder for the board to overreach.

What the Davis-Stirling Act Actually Does

If you live in a California HOA, your rights and your board's obligations are governed by something called the Davis-Stirling Common Interest Development Act. It's a set of state laws that apply to almost every HOA in California, regardless of size, age, or structure.

Many homeowners have never heard of the Davis-Stirling Act, and those who have are often led to believe it's just a vague set of procedural rules. In reality, it's a powerful legal framework that gives you enforceable rights and imposes strict limits on what your board can do.

The Davis-Stirling Act isn't optional. It's the legal framework that controls nearly everything your HOA does: board meetings, elections, document access, architectural review, rules and regulations, funding, maintenance obligations, member discipline, and more.

And if your board violates it, they've broken the law.

The statute begins at Civil Code section 4000 and runs through the 6000s. That might sound overwhelming, but here's the good news: many of the most important protections are grouped in logical sections. And once you understand where those protections live, and what they actually say, you'll stop assuming the board is right just because they act like they are.

That's what this book is going to show you.

For example:

- Want to inspect HOA budgets, contracts, or violation records? That's § 5200.

- Want to dispute a fine or disciplinary hearing? That's § 5855.

- Want to trigger a no-cost dispute process? That's § 5900.

- Want to run for the board and ensure a fair election? That's §§ 5100–5145.

This isn't legal trivia. These are your rights. And your HOA is required to follow them, whether the board understands them or not, and whether they want to or not.

The problem is that most boards don't expect you to know they exist. And most homeowners don't realize how much leverage the Davis-Stirling Act actually gives them.

By the time you finish this book, you will.

Selective Enforcement is Illegal

Selective enforcement is one of the most common complaints homeowners make when it comes to their HOAs. And selective enforcement of the rules is not just unfair, it is illegal. Your HOA doesn't get to pick and choose who the rules apply to. But that's exactly what many of them do.

Here are just a few examples:

- You're ordered to remove hedges or trees in your yard while others have the same landscaping and the board hasn't asked them to remove anything.
- You're denied permission to improve your balcony even though three other homes on your block got permission to make the same improvements to their balconies.
- You get a violation notice for leaving trash cans out a day too long while your neighbor does the same thing every week without consequence.

This isn't a gray area. Courts have ruled that when an HOA enforces a rule arbitrarily or inconsistently, it cannot stand. It's a violation of basic principles of fairness and equal protection.

So what should you do? Document the unequal treatment. Take photos and send them to the board and management company. Then demand that the HOA enforce the rule uniformly or not at all. If they refuse to budge, it might be time to contact an attorney.

WHY YOUR HOA BOARD GETS AWAY WITH SO MUCH AND THE MOST COMMON WAYS THEY ABUSE THEIR POWER

M OST HOMEOWNERS ASSUME that HOA boards are subject to meaningful checks and balances. They believe that rules apply equally, that board members are just neighbors doing their best, and that if something goes wrong, there must be a way to fix it that doesn't involve hurt feelings or egos. And quite frankly, that's the way it should be. But the reality is almost always very different. The structure of most HOAs gives a small group of people broad legal authority with very little oversight, and when that power is abused, the system rarely protects the homeowner unless the homeowner is armed with the right kind of knowledge.

California law gives HOA boards the ability to levy fines, impose rules, suspend privileges, reject improvement requests, deny access to records, and collect money through liens or lawsuits. These powers are real, enforceable, and often misunderstood, even by homeowners who are trying to do everything right. Worse, the processes that claim to protect homeowners are often controlled by the very boards they're meant to limit.

This chapter unpacks what board power really looks like in practice and how bad HOA boards get away with so much abuse. It explains how bad boards exercise control, why so many of their actions go unchallenged, and what legal and procedural blind spots allow bad actors to operate without consequences. In this chapter, therefore, we're showing you the most common abuse patterns that you'll encounter in a California HOA so that you can fully appreciate what you're up against. You may have already seen some of them in your community. The rest of this book will show you how to fight back.

The Myth of Accountability

HOAs love to tell homeowners that their system is fair because it's "self-governed."

They'll tell you that your board was democratically elected. That your voice matters. That if you want to change the rules, all you have to do is run for a seat. And technically, that's true, and on paper, it sounds great. In practice, however, it's a myth because the people who control your HOA, i.e., those three to five board members who set the rules, approve the budgets, and hire the lawyers, are often the only ones actually engaged in the system. And they know it.

The problem usually isn't fraud. It's apathy.

You'd be surprised how many homeowners don't vote. Some don't even open the ballot envelope. In many associations, the biggest challenge isn't defeating the incumbents. It's getting enough members to vote at all. Without enough ballots returned, the association fails to reach quorum, and the current board stays in power by default.

Bad boards count on that. They prefer apathy. Because it means that nobody is paying attention to what they're doing.

Even when elections do happen, boards frequently ignore or mishandle the legal procedures. They change election rules too close to the election date, delay director ballots without cause, or quietly appoint allies mid-term—effectively insulating themselves from challenge.

And when a homeowner objects, the board hides behind the Bylaws. But the truth is, the Bylaws don't override state law.

California Civil Code sections 5100–5145 lay out strict election rules that HOAs must follow, including rules about secret ballots, independent inspectors, open candidate qualifications, and member notices. But most homeowners don't know those rules. And there's no government agency that enforces them.

That's how power gets hoarded in plain sight.

The Perfect Conditions for Abuse

The typical California HOA has three ingredients that make it ripe for abuse:

1. Voter apathy.

2. Legal complexity.

3. Fear of retaliation.

Let's start with voter apathy.

Most homeowners don't show up to meetings. They don't read the budget. They don't return their ballots. They assume the board is acting in good faith. Or, more likely, most of you are just too busy, burned out, or overwhelmed with raising your families to deal with it.

That's not a character flaw. It's human nature. But it creates a vacuum, and bad boards fill that vacuum with control.

Then there's the legal complexity. Even educated, sophisticated homeowners don't know what's in the Davis-Stirling Act. They don't understand what the CC&Rs actually say. And even if they did, the language is dense, jargon-filled, inconsistent, and scattered across multiple documents. Trying to challenge the board without a lawyer feels impossible.

Finally, there's the fear. In a public dispute, you can call a reporter. In a government agency, you can go over someone's head. But in an HOA? There's no neutral authority. No escalation path. No whistleblower protection. The same board that you're accusing of misconduct is the one that decides whether to fine you, restrict your access, or send the HOA's lawyer after you. Board members have egos, and when challenged, bad board members retaliate.

It's no surprise that most homeowners stay quiet even when they know something's wrong.

And for the board, that silence feels like approval.

Power Without Oversight

In most areas of law, someone is watching.

If your employer discriminates against you, you can file with the Department of Fair Employment and Housing. If a landlord violates rent control, you can go to the local housing authority. If a business defrauds you, you can report it to the Attorney General.

But in the HOA world? There's no enforcement agency. No compliance division. No state investigator who steps in when a board violates the law.

And boards know that. The board is counting on the fact that hiring a lawyer is expensive and that most homeowners don't want to bother with it. So, bad HOAs learn very quickly that violating Civil Code requirements has no real consequence unless a homeowner challenges it in court. That's not a theory. That's just the way it is. The Davis-Stirling Act gives you rights, but it doesn't assign anyone to enforce them for you.[1]

So when the board ignores your IDR request, denies your access to documents, or holds a hearing without proper notice, they're not worried about getting caught. Because unless you escalate, no one ever will.

Even HOA lawyers exploit this gap. Some specialize in helping boards "paper over" illegal meetings or retroactively justify improper rule changes. Others threaten homeowners with legal fees they know the board can't actually recover just to scare people into backing down.

It's not just abuse of power. It's abuse of legal ambiguity.

And the only thing that keeps it going is the assumption that you won't do anything about it.

The danger isn't just that boards have power. It's that they often exercise that power in ways that look legitimate on the surface. A rule passed at a meeting. A letter written on official letterhead. A vote taken

---

1. That's not to say that there are no agencies available to enforce federal and state laws when your rights are violated. For example, homeowners facing racial or other forms of discrimination can turn to various state and federal agencies for help.

behind closed doors. To the average homeowner, those acts look "official," which is exactly why bad boards get away with so much abuse.

Many homeowners assume that if something is written in a letter or declared at a meeting, it must be legal. But legality and authority are not the same thing. The Davis-Stirling Act draws very specific boundaries around what boards can and cannot do. When you learn those boundaries, you begin to see how often boards exceed them, and how fragile their authority really is when it's challenged.

HOA boards from Hell thrive in the gray areas between perception and reality. They exploit the fact that most homeowners don't know the statutes, and they count on that ignorance to turn suggestions into rules and rules into weapons. That's why so much of what looks "official" in HOA governance collapses the moment it's put under real legal scrutiny.

Just remember that power without oversight will always tilt toward abuse. And until homeowners start asserting their rights in ways that boards can't ignore, the cycle of selective enforcement, retaliation, and intimidation will continue unchecked.

How HOA Boards Preserve Control

Once a board consolidates power, it doesn't need to cheat or commit fraud to stay in control. All it has to do is exploit the legal tools that were designed to make HOAs function smoothly (but that can just as easily be turned into shields against homeowner pushback).

One example is board appointments. If a director resigns mid-term, most HOA bylaws give the board the authority to appoint a replacement, who will serve out the remainder of the departing board member's term. That makes sense in theory. But in practice, it often becomes a way to stack the board with loyalists who will never question the president. Over time, the board evolves into a closed circle of incumbents who find it easy to keep being reelected.

Another example is election timing. Civil Code section 5100 requires elections for directors at the end of each term. The law, however, doesn't force HOAs to hold elections on a fixed calendar. So bad HOAs will sometimes delay elections.

Boards also exploit member apathy. The law doesn't require directors to step down if no one else runs. And it doesn't invalidate elections when quorum isn't reached. As long as the process is "offered," the board keeps operating even if the majority of homeowners don't participate. This makes HOA elections look fair on paper, while insulating incumbents from actual accountability.

But the most effective tool for maintaining control is legal fatigue. Boards that operate in bad faith don't need to win arguments. They just need to wear you down. Most often, they do this by:

- Ignoring, or playing games, with document requests (until you give up).

- Refusing IDR (until you escalate).

- Holding hearings with vague notices (so you miss them).

- Sending lawyer letters filled with threats (to trigger fear, not action).

And all of it happens within a system that assumes you're the one who has to escalate—file the IDR demand, draft the Civil Code section 5200 demand, start the recall process, or hire a lawyer to correct the board's mistake.

This is how even a small board with minimal understanding of the law can control a community of 100, 200, or 500 homeowners indefinitely.

It's not because they're smart. It's because the system rewards silence. Your silence.

Knowing how or why many bad HOA boards can act with little or no consequence is only half the battle. The other half is recognizing their tactics so that you can spot them early. While every HOA is different, certain abuse patterns show up again and again, from selective enforcement and retaliatory fines, to financial mismanagement and intimidation through legal threats.

In the next section, we'll break down the most common ways boards misuse their power, and how these abuses often hide behind official-sounding procedures. Because the most dangerous abuse isn't the kind that makes headlines. It's the kind that hides behind procedure. Boards know how to dress up retaliation as "decorum," how to deny improvement requests without saying no outright, and how to manipulate the hearing process to punish dissent without ever saying that's what they're doing. On the surface, it all looks legal and above board. But that illusion only works when homeowners don't know what to look for.

The Most Common Way HOAs Abuse Their Power

By the time most homeowners realize that their board is crossing the line, the damage is already done. The letter has been sent. The fine has been posted to their account. The request has been "lost" or "delayed." The meeting has been held without them. Abuse in HOAs rarely starts with one big, obvious move. More often, it presents as a series of small actions that pile up until a homeowner is boxed in.

Some of these tactics are easy to recognize. Others are disguised as procedure, policy, or "just following the rules." The trick is that they look official, and they're often delivered in writing on HOA/management letterhead or by the association's lawyer. That formality gives them weight, even when they're legally baseless.

What follows are the patterns that come up again and again in California HOAs. If you can spot them early, you can stop them before they escalate (or, at the very least, prepare to fight back on your terms).

The Abuse Isn't Always Obvious

Some bad HOA boards are openly hostile, so it's easy to see their abuse points. They interpret every question as a challenge. They yell at homeowners in meetings, send threatening letters (or have the HOA's attorneys send letters for them), impose fines that have no legal basis, and retaliate against homeowners they don't like. In short, they're bullies. Abuse that obvious and open is easy to deal with.

But most abuse isn't that obvious.

It might take the form of selective enforcement, where one homeowner gets cited and another doesn't. Or it might take the form of denied architectural requests, with vague explanation or commentary regarding "aesthetics." Sometimes, it takes the form of the board's refusal to respond to complaints, maintenance requests, or demands for records.

And sometimes, it takes the form of manufactured discipline. Such HOAs love to accuse owners of being "disruptive," "abusive," or "harassing" even when the owner is just asking legitimate questions or raising uncomfortable truths. Why? Because labeling someone a threat gives a bad board cover to restrict access, deny meeting participation, or shut down communication altogether.

In every one of these situations, the board is abusing its authority. But it doesn't look like a screaming match. It looks like procedure. It looks official. It looks legal.

And that's exactly why it works.

Because if you don't understand the limits of the board's authority—or what the law actually requires—you assume they can do whatever they want.

They can't. And starting with the next chapter, we'll show you why.

Patterns of Abuse That You'll See Again and Again

Fortunately, most bad boards aren't very creative. They recycle the same tactics because they work. Here are four of the most common:

1. **Selective Enforcement**. You get a letter from the HOA warning you not to park in your driveway because your garage is being used for storage instead of parking. But your neighbors across the street have been doing the same thing for years and no one's ever said a word to them. Or maybe you're fined for a technical violation that the board has historically ignored, but now suddenly "matters" because you're asking tough questions or attending meetings. When enforcement is inconsistent, targeted, or retaliatory, it's not just unfair, it's illegal.

2. **Abuse of Architectural Control**. You apply to install a small fence in your front yard. The board denies it, citing vague references to "uniformity" or "visual harmony." But several other homes in the community already have fences just like the one you proposed. Or maybe you're told you can't use a certain paint color even though it's already been approved for other homes. This kind of arbitrary enforcement isn't protected by the board's discretion. Under Civil Code section 4765, architectural decisions cannot be unreasonable, arbitrary, or capricious.

3. **Retaliatory Enforcement**. You start attending meetings, filing complaints, or organizing neighbors—and suddenly, the board becomes very interested in enforcing rules you've never been cited for before. You're told there's a hearing scheduled about your garage use, or noise, or landscaping, i.e., something minor, something you've never been warned about until now. Then comes the violation letter. Maybe even a fine. Or the board tells you that your speaking time at meetings will be "limited for decorum." This kind of selective escalation is textbook retaliation. It's not always dramatic, but it's always calculated. It's how bad boards try to intimidate owners without triggering obvious legal red flags.

4. **Legal Intimidation**. The HOA's attorney sends you a letter accusing you of harassment or interference with the HOA's

vendors. You're even accused of workplace harassment. The language is vague, the threat is broad, and the goal is simple: to scare you into silence. These letters often cite no enforceable rule. But they work because they're scary and because most homeowners don't know how to respond. They're just scared of being sued.

These tactics only work when no one pushes back. And most homeowners don't because they don't know how. That's what the next chapter will start to fix.

CAN MY HOA ENFORCE RULES THAT CONFLICT WITH THE LAW?

The answer is no. Your HOA can't enforce rules that conflict with federal, state, or local law. Under California law, HOA rules and CC&Rs are enforceable, but only to the extent they don't violate higher legal authority.

That said, it's important to understand what "conflict" really means. Just because something is legal in California doesn't mean your HOA has to allow it. In fact, HOAs are often allowed to adopt stricter rules than federal, state, or local law, especially when it comes to things like parking, smoking, or architectural standards.

But if the HOA passes a rule that directly violates your legal rights, or tries to enforce something the law says they can't, like banning you from having artificial turf or having a dog, restricting EV chargers, or blocking access to common areas without due process, then that's where they cross the line and their authority ends.

So yes, your HOA's governing documents have legal weight, but they can't override or directly conflict with the law, and they can't take away rights that the law explicitly protects.

UNDERSTANDING YOUR RIGHTS UNDER THE DAVIS-STIRLING ACT

M ANY HOA MEMBERS treat HOA disputes like a matter of opinion—one person's interpretation of the rules versus another's. They think the board's decisions are final because the board "runs the HOA." They assume that if the board made a rule, it must be enforceable, and that if the board denies a request, that's the end of the road.

But that's not how HOA law works in California.

Every HOA in the state, no matter how big or small, new or old, is governed by a specific body of state law called the Davis-Stirling Common Interest Development Act. These aren't recommendations or best practices. They're binding legal standards. And when your HOA violates them, it's not just a bad decision, it's a legal failure.

Most homeowners don't realize that the Davis-Stirling Act, and not just their governing documents, controls what their HOA can and can't do. The Davis-Stirling Act doesn't just supplement your HOA's governing documents. It overrides them when there's a conflict, and it controls the procedures your board must follow, the rights you have as a homeowner, and what happens when the board ignores those rights.

This chapter will walk you through the parts of Davis-Stirling that matter most:

- What your HOA is required to do under the law.

- Where boards most often overstep.

- How to recognize violations when they're dressed up to look "official."

Because once you stop assuming the board's version of the rules is correct, you can start relying on what actually is.

The Davis-Stirling Act: The Six Categories That Matter Most

The Davis-Stirling Act isn't one statute. It's a full division of the California Civil Code, beginning at section 4000 and extending through the 6000s. The Act covers nearly every aspect of how homeowners associations are supposed to operate, from board meetings and elections, to maintenance responsibilities, budgeting, rule enforcement, and dispute resolution.

And while the statute can be full of legalese and needlessly complicated jargon, some of it is easy to follow, especially when you know where to look. But for purposes of this book, we're going to focus on the sections that most directly affect you as a homeowner. These aren't the only rights the Davis-Stirling Act gives you, but they're the ones boards most often ignore or violate:

- **Access to Information** *(Civil Code §§ 5200-5250)*. You have the right to inspect nearly all of your HOA's internal records, including financials, contracts, violation logs, budgets, and meeting minutes. Your board doesn't get to say no. And, except for the membership list, they don't get to ask why you want the documents.

- **Annual Disclosures and Financial Reporting** *(Civil Code §§ 5300, 5310, 5565, 5500–5551)*. Each year, your HOA is required to give you a set of mandatory reports and disclosures, including budget summaries, reserve study updates, insurance details, and notices about your rights. If they don't, or if they send vague substitutes, they've violated the law.

- **Member Discipline and Due Process** *(Civil Code §§ 5850–5855)*. Before your HOA can fine you, suspend your access, or take formal action against you, they must follow a legally required set of procedures (e.g., providing notice, opportunity to be heard, and specific findings). If they skip steps or hold sham hearings, the fines or other discipline won't be legal.

- **Dispute Resolution (IDR/ADR)** *(Civil Code §§ 5900–5965).* Your HOA must participate in internal dispute resolution (IDR) if you request it. And in some cases, you and your HOA must also attempt to engage in alternative dispute resolution (ADR), almost always in the form of mediation, before you can file suit against each other.

- **Board Elections and Member Voting** *(Civil Code §§ 5100–5145).* The election of directors must follow strict secret-ballot procedures, including timelines, notices, and neutral inspectors. Boards that ignore or manipulate these rules are breaking the law.

- **Assessments, Maintenance, and Reserves** *(Civil Code §§ 4775, 5300, 5550, 5600–5705).* You have the right to know what your HOA is supposed to maintain, how reserve funding is calculated, when special assessments are allowed, and how emergency repairs are justified. The board doesn't get to spend your money in the dark.

These categories aren't isolated. They overlap constantly. But once you understand how Davis-Stirling is structured, and how your board tries to sidestep it, you'll start seeing patterns.

And once you see the patterns, you'll know how to fight back.

Breaking Down The Six Categories That Matter Most

The Davis-Stirling Act is expansive. But some rights matter more than others when it comes to day-to-day power struggles between homeowners and their boards.

In the last section, we outlined six key categories of homeowner rights under the Davis-Stirling Act where California law gives you real leverage and where boards most often cross the line.

What follows is a deeper dive into each of those six areas, where we'll discuss:

- What the law actually says.

- What the board is supposed to do.

- How HOAs from Hell fall short.

- What you can do about it (i.e., how you can respond).

Understanding those six categories is the foundation for everything that follows. They aren't abstract principles. They're the pressure points where boards most often break the law and where homeowners have the greatest ability to push back. As you move into the next chapters, you'll see each area unpacked in detail, where I'll provide you with statutes, strategies, and examples you'll need to spot violations and turn them into leverage.

Use Civil Code § 5200 To Access HOA Records Like a Pro

While California Civil Code § 5200 gives homeowners the legal right to inspect and copy a wide range of HOA records, most homeowners have no idea just how broad that right really is.

Among other HOA-related documents, you're entitled to see:

- Bank statements.
- Canceled checks.
- Credit card statements.
- General ledgers.
- Balance sheets.
- Income and expense reports.
- Reserve account records.
- Vendor contracts and invoices.
- Insurance policies.
- Spending receipts.
- Reimbursement records.
- Tax returns.

Basically, if the HOA paid for it, approved it, or relied on it to justify how they've been spending your HOA dues, then you're almost always entitled to see and copy it.

And this isn't just about catching fraud. It's about ensuring transparency, protecting your investment, and keeping your board honest.

YOUR LEGAL RIGHT
TO HOA RECORDS
IN CALIFORNIA

I NFORMATION IS POWER, and in an HOA, it's often the only power a homeowner can exercise without going to court. Fortunately, in this regard, the Davis-Stirling Act actually arms HOA members with a clearly stated legal right to inspect a broad range of association records, including a wide array of financial documents, invoices, meeting minutes, vendor information, and contracts.

But boards don't always comply. In fact, more often than not, boards violate both the letter and the spirit of the law intended to keep homeowners informed of their HOA's business dealings. Some delay or ignore document requests entirely. Others claim records don't exist, or that you're not entitled to see them, or that "the board is still reviewing the matter internally." These excuses are almost never valid. And when they come from an HOA with something to hide, they're often used to cover up wrongdoing.

This chapter breaks down what you're allowed to see, when the HOA must produce it, and how to force compliance when the board refuses. It also explains what redactions are allowed, what penalties apply for illegal withholdings, and how to make your request bulletproof from the start. If you want to know what your HOA is really doing behind the scenes, this is where to begin.

Records are Power

If you've ever asked your HOA for records and been ignored, stalled, overcharged, or gaslit, then you're not alone. Most HOAs don't comply with Civil Code section 5200 voluntarily. They hide behind excuses.

They pretend not to understand the request. They demand outrageous fees. And sometimes, they simply stonewall.

Then, when that gets old, the board claims that they'll "check with management," promises a follow-up, then vanishes. Or, if they do respond, it's often with a cherry-picked handful of documents, no explanation as to what documents they excluded (either because they don't have them, or they simply didn't turn them over), a bunch of redactions that they never explain, and a bloated invoice.

In HOA disputes, transparency equals accountability, while secrecy creates opportunity for abuse. Secrecy enables unchecked expenses, cozy vendor deals, late reserve deposits, reserve fund abuse, and even hidden conflicts of interest, self-dealing, and other breaches of fiduciary duty. Your HOA is managing your money, and the law says that you have a legal right to see where every dollar goes.

HOAs from Hell relish operating in the dark. That's why they often try to withhold information. They know that most homeowners won't push too hard to get documents, so if they make it difficult, many curious homeowners will give up. They count on confusion, on intimidation, and on the belief that HOA documents are somehow "internal" or off-limits.

But California law says otherwise. California Civil Code section 5200 gives homeowners powerful access rights. The law is detailed, enforceable, and loaded with real penalties when HOAs don't comply. But the statute only works if you use it correctly, and unfortunately, most homeowners don't. *I hope that this book helps solve that problem.*

In this chapter, I will explain:

- What records you're entitled to inspect.

- How to request them properly.

- What timelines the board must follow.

- What happens when the board fails to produce documents.

- How this right can unlock proof of retaliation, fraud, favoritism, or financial abuse.

You don't need to prove wrongdoing to request the records to which you're legally entitled. And with one minor exception (related to the membership list), you don't need to explain *why* you want the records. You just have to ask for them correctly. And that's what this chapter will show you how to do.

What You're Entitled to Inspect and Copy

The Davis-Stirling Act doesn't just say you have a right to "records." Civil Code section 5200 is anything *but* vague. It spells out exactly which types of records homeowners are legally entitled to inspect and copy, and if you read the statute carefully, you'll see just how broad that list actually is.

If the association has the document, and it doesn't fall into one of a couple of extremely narrow exceptions, you're entitled to see it and copy it. No justification required.

The following represents a comprehensive, and carefully curated, list of the documents that you're entitled to see and copy. This isn't a complete list, but it's the most useful one that you'll find:

- Membership list, along with email addresses (for those who have not affirmatively opted out) (Civ. Code, §§ 5200(a)(9); 5220).

- Governing documents (Civ. Code, § 5200(a)(11)).

- Monthly and annual bank statements (Civ. Code, § 5200(a)(13)).

- Balance sheets (Civ. Code, § 5200(a)(3)(A)).

- Income and expense statements (Civ. Code, § 5200(a)(3)(B)).

- Canceled checks (Civ. Code, § 5200(a)(13)).

- Check registers (Civ. Code, §§ 5200(a)(10), 5200(a)(13)).

- The general ledger (Civ. Code, § 5200(a)(3)(D)).

- Credit card statements (Civ. Code, §§ 5200(a)(10), 5200(a)(13)).

- Purchase orders approved by the HOA (Civ. Code, § 5200(a)(13)).

- Invoices for services rendered to the HOA (Civ. Code, § 5200(a)(13)).

- Reimbursement requests submitted to the HOA (Civ. Code, § 5200(a)(13)).

- Certificates of insurance for vendors or contractors (Civ. Code, § 5200(a)(4)).

- Current and prior master insurance policies (Civ. Code, § 5200(a)(4)).

- Declaration pages for current-year insurance policies (Civ. Code, § 5200(a)(4)).

- Notices of all board meetings, including executive sessions (Civ. Code, § 5200(a)(8)).

- Agendas for all board meetings, including executive sessions (Civ. Code, § 5200(a)(8)).

- Minutes for all open board meetings (Civ. Code, § 5200(a)(8)).

- Annual budget report, including the pro forma budget or summary, reserve funding plan, and funding methodology (Civ. Code, §§ 5200(a)(1), 5320(b)).

- Annual policy statement, including the notice of right to receive board meeting minutes, assessment collection policy, and fine schedule (Civ. Code, §§ 5200(a)(1), 5310(b), 5320(b)).

- Management agent disclosures (Civ. Code, §§ 5375, 5380).

- Full reserve studies (Civ. Code, § 5320(b)).

- Reserve account balances and records of reserve fund expenditures (Civ. Code, § 5200(a)(7)).

- All signed contracts not covered by legal privilege (Civ. Code, § 5200(a)(4)).

- Budget comparisons (Civ. Code, § 5200(a)(3)(C)).

- Federal and state tax returns (Civ. Code, § 5200(a)(6)).

- Election rules and board qualification criteria (Civ. Code, § 5200(a)(11)).

Now, I previously alluded to an exception involving your right to inspect and copy the membership list for your HOA—i.e., the list of the names, addresses, and email addresses of your fellow HOA members. While you're entitled to request the membership list, the board may legally withhold it if it *reasonably* believes that you requested the list for an improper purpose, such as harassment, commercial solicitation, or disrupting HOA operations.

Let's take a minute to unpack what "harassment" or "improper purpose" actually means. Wanting the membership list so that you can criticize the board's leadership, organize a recall, or communicate with your neighbors about board misconduct does *not* ever qualify as harassment, improper use, or disruption. It might very well disrupt operations, but not in the way the law uses that term. On the contrary, that kind of grassroots organizing is exactly what membership access laws were designed to support.

The bottom line is that the improper-purpose exception is narrow. It applies to situations like commercial solicitation, threats, or fraud, not to legitimate homeowner advocacy.

What to Put in Your 5200 Document Demand and Why It Matters

A 5200 demand isn't just about requesting specific documents (like those described above), nor is it a matter of mere formality. If done correctly, it creates the legal foundation for penalties, attorneys' fees, and court enforcement. But if it's vague or improperly cited, you've just given the board free cover to ignore your request, engage in bad faith gamesmanship, or at the very least, substantially delay their compliance.

The more clearly and strategically you write your request, the harder it becomes for the HOA to claim confusion or create roadblocks. And when they do try to stall, a properly written request will be your best evidence in court.

You'll maximize your chances of success if, at minimum, your "5200 document demand" includes all of the following:

- **A clear statement regarding who you are**. Provide your name, address, and email address. Boards love to delay by pretending they can't confirm who's making the request.

- **A list of each category of documents as a separate, numbered item**. The more granular your request, the harder it is for them to "accidentally" omit something. Use some or all of the listed items that I provided above.

- **The specific Civil Code section next to each document category**. This makes it much more difficult for the board to claim they "didn't know what you meant" or were confused about whether you had a right to the document category in question. *It also not-so-subtly reinforces the notion that your requests are backed by enforceable state law*. Again, you can refer to the list that I provided above.

- **A hard deadline for the HOA's compliance: 5 days for the membership list, 10 business days for current-year fiscal**

documents, 30 calendar days for the rest. This prevents the board from pretending that they didn't know the timeline.

- **Specifics regarding your preferred format**. If you want digital files, say so. If the HOA has the documents in electronic form, they're required to give them to you that way. While your HOA can't charge you for copying or printing them out (as a means of harassment), they can charge you their "direct cost of producing the copy of a record in [an] electronic format."

- **A statement "reminding" the HOA that you're entitled to inspect or receive copies at their direct or actual cost**. If you want to inspect in person, they can't charge you a dime. If you want copies, they can only charge you their "direct and actual cost of copying and mailing" the requested documents. While your HOA has to inform you of their estimated actual costs *before* they proceed with copying the documents, if you approve them to go ahead, they can require you to pre-pay those costs before they provide the documents.

- **If your demand includes a request for the membership list, a statement that your request is being made for a proper purpose related to your membership rights**. This will prevent the board from stalling the process by waiting out the relevant timeline, and then seeking "clarification" about your purpose. So, for example, if you're requesting the membership list, you might include a footnote after that itemized request that says something along the lines of *"I'm requesting the membership list so that I can communicate with my fellow HOA members about matters relating to the management and operations of this HOA."*

- **A request that the HOA disclose any categories of docu-ments they are withholding, redacting, or deeming privi-leged, along with the statutory basis**. This is required under

Civil Code section 5215(d), but only if the member explicitly requests it. So *always* do that up front in your initial demand.

- **A statement that for the purposes of your 5200 demand, each line item will be treated as a separate violation**. The purpose of this is to maximize the statutory penalties, which the statute lists as "up to" $500 *per request*. In other words, let's say that you're asking for 20 separate categories of documents. Rather than sending 20 separate 5200 demands, each containing one category, you're combining them into one letter. But you're also reserving your right to request up to $500 *per request* in statutory penalties. If your HOA were to refuse to produce any of the 20 categories of documents, you'd be entitled to up to $10,000 in statutory penalties.

Your 5200 demand should be sent via certified mail, FedEx, or any other nationally recognized courier that requires a signature upon receipt, *as well as via email.*

Following that structure can make all the difference. It locks in statutory deadlines and boxes the HOA into a corner if they don't comply. And if your HOA still fails to comply by producing all of the records that you requested, you'll have everything you need to move toward legal enforcement.

HOA Delays and Gamesmanship

Once your 5200 demand is out the door, you are under no obligation to extend deadlines or wait around for management companies, boards, or insurance adjusters to "look into it" or investigate your demand. Civil Code section 5200 provides clear and enforceable deadlines regardless of whether or not your HOA is aware of them, and regardless of whether or not your HOA wants more time to review your demand.

So when bad HOAs don't want to comply, they don't usually just say "no" outright. Instead, they stall, pretend to cooperate, or deliver a partial response to give the appearance of compliance. These tactics are strategic, not accidental, and they're designed to exhaust you.

Here are the most common forms of gamesmanship to watch for:

- **"We're checking with management."/"We'll get back to you."** These phrases are HOA speak for *"We're buying time."* Don't be fooled by polite acknowledgments or vague assurances. If the HOA hasn't produced the records by the applicable statutory deadlines, then they're in violation no matter how nicely they stall. Remember, Civil Code section 5200 imposes strict timeframes on the production of documents—i.e., 5 business days for membership lists, 10 business days for current fiscal-year financial documents, and 30 calendar days for all the remaining categories of documents. There is no extension for "we're checking with our management company."

- **Bogus "privilege" delays**. Similar to the prior example, many HOAs try to buy time by telling the homeowner that they have to check with the HOA's attorneys, either because they're uncertain regarding your rights to certain categories of documents that you demanded (which is why you should provide those statutory citations offered above), or because your demand includes documents that the board thinks might be privileged. Neither represents a valid excuse to miss the statutory deadlines.[1]

- **Producing some, but not all, of the records while offering no explanation**. This is one of the most common forms of abuse involving 5200 demands. Let's say that your 5200 demand encompasses 15 of the categories referenced above, and that compliance by the HOA would yield 500 or more pages of documents. If your HOA provides you with a 300, 400, or even

---

1. FYI, while attorney fee agreements are usually considered privileged documents, in the HOA sphere, they are not. Homeowners have a right to review unredacted copies of any fee/retainer agreements between their HOA and the HOA's attorneys.

500-page zip file, the only way that you can determine if the HOA has complied with your document demand is to go over every page of the production and then figure out for yourself what, if anything, is missing. That process could take hours and hours of your time. And when HOAs from Hell play that omission game, they do so because they know how long it will take you to figure out what might be missing, and they're hoping that you won't bother. It's a form of obstruction, not a clerical oversight, and it represents a calculated effort to punish home-owners like you for exercising your rights. That is the reason why you should explicitly cite Civil Code section 5215(d) in your 5200 demand. You want to legally obligate the HOA to provide you with an explanation as to every document that they have withheld (either because the document doesn't exist, or because they're intentionally holding it back) or redacted. By triggering that obligation, you may be able to prevent the HOA from engaging that way at all, but at the very least, you'll have great evidence to support your demand for maximum statutory penalties.

- **Abusive redaction**. Redactions are permitted in narrow circum-stances, primarily when dealing with privileged, personal, or sensitive information. But boards often black out entire sections of documents with no justification at all. That's not protection, it's obstruction. And once again, the reason why you should include the citation to 5215(d) is to require your HOA to explain the scope and basis of each redaction made.

- **Billing abuse**. One of the most common forms of HOA games-manship in response to a 5200 demand is billing abuse. They'll send a bloated invoice to discourage you from pursuing the full set of records to which you're entitled. This tactic isn't about cost recovery, it's about deterrence. Your HOA is entitled to charge you for: (a) their actual and direct copying costs (assuming that the documents you demanded are not already stored electronically); (b) up to $10 per hour for redaction of those narrowly tailored documents that are rightfully deemed privileged or sensitive; and (c) a *reasonable* hourly fee for organizing paper records if they exist in hard copy form. That's it. Your HOA may *not* charge for "research time," "administrative costs," "processing fees," or "manager review."

Most homeowners think of record requests as optional, as if the board is doing them a favor by supplying the requested documents. That's exactly the mindset your HOA wants you to have. But the truth is the opposite. Your board is required by law to give you those records. And if they don't? You can force their compliance and make them pay for their delay.

Legal Enforcement: What Happens if Your HOA Ignores Your Demand?

If your HOA fails to comply with your 5200 demand, whether they ignore it outright, drag their feet, or play games with partial production, they've violated California law. And that opens the door to legal enforcement.

Under Civil Code section 5235, as well as Code of Civil Procedure section 1085, any homeowner who submits a valid 5200 demand can take formal legal action against their HOA to compel compliance. That legal action can come in three distinct forms, each of which carries substantial consequences for the HOA:

1. File a Writ of Mandate.

2. File a lawsuit in "regular" court.

3. File a small claims lawsuit.

File a Writ of Mandate

A writ of mandate under Code of Civil Procedure section 1085 is an efficient option available to you when you're seeking to force the HOA to comply with its legal obligations, but not otherwise seeking monetary damages. If you're actually seeking monetary damages, the Writ process isn't the best option.[2]

The Writ process is typically much faster than traditional litigation because it's supposed to dispense with most of the litigation-related processes, such as discovery.[3] Generally, you would initiate the process by filing a Writ (a glorified motion). The court will set a hearing date, and between the time of the Writ's filing and the hearing, the HOA will file an Opposition, and you will then have the opportunity to file a Reply to the HOA's Opposition. That's it.

In the Writ process, you're asking the court to command the HOA to do something it is legally required to do, namely, produce the records listed in the 5200 demand.

Upon prevailing, you will be entitled to: (a) an order compelling the HOA to produce the missing documents; (b) civil penalties of up to $500 per request; and (c) attorneys' fees and costs. If the HOA wins, it is not automatically entitled to its attorneys' fees and costs unless the court determines that the Writ was "frivolous, unreasonable, or without foundation." That's a high bar to meet, so it rarely happens.

Caution. The Writ process might trigger the ADR requirement contained in Civil Code section 5930. Not all courts agree with that because of some provisions in the Government Code and the Code of Civil Procedure. But until the appellate court addresses the split in authority, it is a distinct

---

2. Seeking statutory penalties and attorneys' fees does not constitute seeking monetary damages.

3. I say "supposed to" because some judges like to treat Writs as if they're "mini-lawsuits," and thus order parties to mandatory settlement conferences and case management conferences. While none of that is remotely contemplated in the applicable statutes, if you draw a judge who treats Writs that way, you're just going to have to live with it.

possibility. The safe bet, therefore, is to make a formal demand for ADR under Civil Code section 5930.

File a Lawsuit

You can also file a standard civil lawsuit in the superior court against the HOA for violating section 5235. A lot of people choose this path when they have additional claims to pursue (other than just compelling production of documents following a 5200 demand) or the HOA's failure to produce documents caused actual damages (e.g., failure to produce documents related to fire disclosures cost you the sale of your condo).

Taking this route might require you to jump through the ADR hoop if any of your claims are considered enforcement (of the governing documents) claims and you're either seeking *only* declaratory, injunctive, or writ relief, or if you're seeking one or more of those claims, as well as money damages of less than $12,500. Most cases do not fall under the requirement, but if yours does, you can't skip the ADR process.[4]

Litigation is very expensive, and if it goes to trial, it will take a long time (at least 2-3 years) to resolve.

Upon prevailing, you will be entitled to: (a) an order compelling the HOA to produce the missing documents; (b) civil penalties of up to $500 per request; (c) any other monetary damages that you prove; (d) orders from the court related to other claims; and (e) attorneys' fees and costs. If the HOA wins on the 5200 portion of your case, it is not automatically entitled to its attorneys' fees and costs unless the court determines that the Writ was "frivolous, unreasonable, or without foundation." The HOA may, however, be entitled to its attorneys' fees and costs incurred in defending against your non-5200-related claims.

---

4. The ADR process for HOA-related disputes is described in detail in Chapter 7 of this book.

File a Small Claims Lawsuit

By far, the fastest and least expensive route to go is to file in small claims court. This is usually preferable if your 5200 was fairly limited and straightforward, and didn't require you to obtain the advice or help of an attorney.

There is no ADR requirement associated with small claims cases, so that's not an issue.

And if you prevail, you're entitled to an order from the court compelling the HOA to produce the missing documents and civil penalties of up to $500 per request. You are not, however, entitled to your attorneys' fees and costs even if you consulted with an attorney to help you prepare the 5200 demand or for the small claims case.

All three of those options are valid, and depending on your circumstances, any of those options could be the right decision for you. The most important thing is that you know these tools exist. Boards count on homeowners not following through. But if your 5200 demand was properly written and your HOA still refuses to comply, you have every right to take them to court and make them pay.

Can My HOA Choose Not to Send Out the Annual Disclosures?

Every year, your HOA is legally required to provide you with a package of disclosures. And if they're not doing it? That's a problem.

Under the Davis-Stirling Act, your board must send out an annual disclosure package that includes the budget, a reserve funding plan, a summary of the HOA's insurance coverage, and key financial statements. They must also send out a variety of notices about enforcement policies, internal dispute resolution, and more.

These disclosures are not optional. They're required by law to help homeowners make informed decisions and hold boards accountable.

And if your HOA skips or delays these disclosures, it's not just frustrating, it's against the law. And if your board does fail to provide the mandatory disclosures, you'll be entitled to file a complaint, withhold certain permissions, or even challenge future board decisions that weren't made transparently.

So check your mailbox (or your inbox). If your board hasn't sent out the required package by the deadline, it's time to call them out.

ANNUAL DISCLOSURES, FINANCIAL REPORTING, AND RESERVE STUDIES

I F YOU'VE EVER looked at your HOA dues and wondered where that money actually goes, you're not alone. Homeowners are expected to pay monthly assessments, fund reserves, and cover special assessments when they arise. Many HOAs, however, prefer to keep their members in the dark about how those amounts are calculated, who decides how they're spent, or whether the board is managing its finances responsibly.

Fortunately, the Davis-Stirling Act requires every California HOA to prepare and distribute a detailed set of financial and policy-related disclosures each year. These aren't suggestions or best practices. They're mandatory reports governed by specific timelines, formats, and content requirements. The annual budget, reserve study (or reserve summary), assessment disclosures, delinquency policies, and insurance summaries all fall under this framework. And if the HOA fails to provide them, or provides misleading information, the HOA, and under certain circumstances, even individual board members, may be held liable.

This chapter explains what your HOA must disclose, when those disclosures are due, and what to look for when reviewing them. It also breaks down what rights you have when the board overspends, underfunds reserves, hides liabilities, or pushes through emergency assessments without notice. You're not just paying dues. You're funding a business. And you have every right to see how that business is run.

What Financial Disclosures HOAs Are Legally Required to Make Each Year

Every year, your HOA is legally required to prepare and distribute a package of financial disclosures. These aren't optional, and they're not subject to board discretion. Civil Code sections 5300 and 5310 spell out exactly what must be included, when it must be sent, and what consequences the board could face if they ignore their duties.

This package is typically called the "Annual Budget Report" and the "Annual Policy Statement." Together, these documents form the backbone of HOA transparency. They're supposed to show how your money is being handled, how the board plans to fund future repairs, and what policies govern your rights and responsibilities as a member.

Here's what the law actually requires.

The Annual Budget Report

The Budget Report must be distributed to all homeowners between 30 and 90 days before the start of the HOA's fiscal year. In most associations, that means it's due sometime in the fall. Too many boards, however, get the timing wrong, and thus missed deadlines are not uncommon.

Under Civil Code section 5300, the report must include all of the following:

- A detailed operating budget showing estimated revenue and expenses for the coming year.

- A summary of the association's reserves (including the current balance, estimated remaining life of each major component, and the percentage funded figure described later in this chapter).

- A statement as to whether the board plans to defer any repairs or replacements.

- A statement of how the reserve study affects the HOA's budget and whether any special assessments or loans are expected.

- A disclosure about the procedure for handling monetary defaults (i.e., collections).

- A summary of the HOA's insurance policies, including coverage types, limits, and deductibles.

- A statement about how members can request full copies of the reserve study and insurance policies.

Each of these items has specific formatting and content requirements under the Civil Code. For example, the reserve summary must be in the statutory format laid out under Civil Code section 5565, and the insurance summary must use the precise disclaimers required by Civil Code section 5300(b)(9).

I've included a table summarizing these disclosures at the end of this chapter.

The Annual Policy Statement

In addition to the Budget Report, the HOA must also send out an Annual Policy Statement, which provides homeowners with a snapshot of key rights, procedures, and internal rules. These include:

- The process for homeowners to request HOA records.

- The mailing address for official communications.

- Discipline policies.

- Architectural guidelines and procedures.

- Procedures for resolving disputes through internal dispute resolution (IDR).

- How the HOA handles overnight delivery and posting of notices.

- Statements regarding secondary addresses for notices, board meeting schedules, and other procedural rights.

Like the Budget Report, this Policy Statement must also be distributed between 30 and 90 days before the start of the fiscal year. These deadlines are mandatory, and courts have consistently treated them as enforceable, not aspirational.

I've included a table summarizing these disclosures at the end of this chapter.

What if the Board Doesn't Send Those Reports?

Failure to distribute those disclosures constitutes negligence, and quite possibly, a breach of fiduciary duty. In many cases, it signals deeper problems: mismanagement of funds, lack of planning, or an effort to conceal financial issues. Boards that skip these reports, or distribute incomplete ones, open themselves up to legal action.

Homeowners are not powerless in these situations. If your board hasn't provided these required reports, you can send a formal written demand, bring the issue to the membership, or explore legal remedies that compel compliance or impose penalties.

Insurance Requirements and Why They Matter

Insurance is one of the least understood but most important obligations of an HOA. California law does not require HOAs to carry most types of insurance that you probably assume they're required to carry. In fact, the Davis-Stirling Act mandates only one kind outright: fidelity bond coverage. Civil Code section 5806 requires associations to maintain fidelity bond insurance that protects against fraud or theft committed by anyone handling HOA funds, including directors, officers, employees, and managing agents. The minimum amount must equal or exceed the combined total of the association's reserves, plus three months of regular assessments.

Most people are shocked to hear that, especially those who live in multi-family housing (e.g., condominiums), where HOAs own a lot of common area. That shock is completely understandable. After all, it seems obvious that the law would require coverage for fire, water damage, or liability in shared spaces precisely because the risks are so obvious and the potential losses so large. But outside of the fidelity bond requirement, the Davis-Stirling Act is dead silent.

The good news is that homeowners usually don't have to panic. In almost all cases, your HOA's CC&Rs already require your HOA to carry robust coverage for property and liability risks even though the statute does not. In practice, a lot of boards comply because their CC&Rs obligate them to, and because lenders won't finance a condo purchase without proof of that coverage.[1]

To be clear, even though the Davis-Stirling Act may not require HOAs to carry liability, earthquake, or flood insurance, most sets of CC&Rs do. The exact mix varies by community. Problems arise, however, when an HOA makes a choice not to carry the coverages required in its CC&Rs because that failure can expose every homeowner to substantial (and unnecessary) financial risk. If a board ignores those obligations, lenders may refuse to finance or refinance units in the development, insurers may balk at covering individual owners, and one major uncovered loss— such as following a major fire or earthquake—could trigger financially devastating special assessments. In other words, the coverage may be written into your CC&Rs, but it only protects you if the board actually maintains it.

One other statute, Civil Code section 5800, matters here. It does not require any specific coverage, but it does protect volunteer directors and officers from personal liability if the HOA maintains insurance

---

1. Still, the fact that the protection comes from your governing documents and not from state law is an important distinction, and a reminder of why reviewing your HOA's insurance disclosures is essential.

that covers the type of claim involved. If your board cuts corners and doesn't maintain appropriate coverage, directors and officers could lose that liability shield. That creates a dangerous dynamic where decisions may be driven by fear of personal exposure instead of the community's best interests.

For homeowners, the takeaway is simple. Review your CC&Rs to determine what insurance your HOA is required to carry, and then review your annual insurance disclosures to confirm that your HOA is abiding by their legal obligations. Reviewing these items is critical to ensuring that gaps in coverage don't result in costing you money later.

The Reserve Study Requirement And Why It Matters

Every HOA in California is legally required to prepare a reserve study every three years. This isn't a budgeting suggestion or a best practice. It's a legal obligation under the Davis-Stirling Act, and it exists for one reason: to make sure your HOA doesn't run out of money when the roof needs replacing, the elevators break down, or the plumbing fails.

Many homeowners have never seen their HOA's reserve study. Many have no idea it exists. But it's one of the most important documents in the entire HOA system because it determines how and when major repairs will be funded and whether special assessments might be needed to cover the cost.

What is a Reserve Study?

A reserve study is a formal report prepared by a licensed professional that assesses the long-term repair and replacement needs of the HOA's major components. It includes:

- An inventory of all major components the HOA is responsible for maintaining.

- The estimated useful life of each component.

- The estimated remaining useful life of each component.

- The estimated cost to repair or replace each component.

- A funding plan showing how the HOA will accumulate enough reserves to meet these future obligations.

This study isn't about routine maintenance. It's about capital repairs to your HOA's major components, like re-roofing buildings, resurfacing roads, replacing balconies, or replacing pool equipment. If the board isn't planning ahead, the costs hit homeowners all at once in the form of steep special assessments.

How Often Does Your HOA Have to Update the Study?

California law requires every HOA to update its reserve planning regularly. This does *not* mean every few years, but rather every year.

At minimum, the board must:

- **Conduct a physical inspection of the major components at least once every three years**. Civil Code section 5550(a) requires this inspection to be performed with competence and diligence. There are no longer any exemptions for small HOAs. The visual inspection requirement applies to all associations if the cost of repairing or replacing the major components equals or exceeds 50 percent of the HOA's gross budget (excluding reserves).

- **Review the reserve study annually**, including the reserve account balance and the funding plan. The board is required to consider whether the current level of assessments is sufficient, and if not, to implement necessary adjustments.

- **Disclose a summary of the reserve funding plan to all homeowners each year**. That summary, called the "Assessment and Reserve Funding Disclosure Summary," must be included in the Annual Budget Report. It contains key figures such as the current reserve balance, estimated replacement costs, and the HOA's "percent funded."

Boards that skip these updates or distribute inaccurate summaries are not just being sloppy. They're breaching their fiduciary duties and placing the entire community at risk of future financial hardship.

Why This Matters to Homeowners

Reserve studies directly affect your wallet.

If the board underestimates costs or fails to follow the funding plan, homeowners will, at some point in the future, be blindsided by large special assessments when inevitable repairs/replacements arise. Far too many HOAs in California have dramatically underfunded reserve accounts, often holding less than 50% of what's actually needed (this is the "percent funded" number that is disclosed every year).

The reserve study also controls what gets disclosed in the Annual Budget Report. That includes:

- The current reserve balance.

- The percent funded based on current contributions.

- Whether any repairs will be deferred.

- Whether the board expects to take out a loan or levy a special assessment.

If the board doesn't have an up-to-date reserve study, those disclosures will be inaccurate or missing entirely.

Some boards try to avoid updating their reserve studies because the numbers make them look bad. That's not just negligent. It's against the law.

Understanding the "Percent Funded" Figure And Why It's Often Misleading

The ABCs of the Percent Funded Number

One of the most important numbers in your HOA's financial disclosures is the "percent funded" figure. It appears in both the Assessment and Reserve Funding Disclosure Summary (which is included in the Annual Budget Report) and in the full reserve study itself. And while it may look like just another percentage on the page, it's actually one of the clearest indicators of your HOA's financial health (provided, of course, that it's being calculated and disclosed honestly).

The "percent funded" number provides a snapshot in time of how well the HOA is positioned to meet its future obligations regarding the repairs/replacements of its major components. In plain English: it tells you whether your HOA is on track to have enough money set aside when it's time to repair or replace the big-ticket items, like the roof, the roads, the plumbing, or the balconies.

Here's a simplified example:

Suppose your HOA has only one major component—a roof—and that roof has a projected useful life of 10 years and a replacement cost of $1 million. As part of the reserve study, the preparer will calculate how much the HOA should have accumulated at each point along that 10-year timeline to remain on track. So if you're in year 7, and the roof is 70% through its useful life, the reserve study will estimate that the HOA should have roughly 70% of the replacement cost set aside at that point, or about $700,000. If the HOA has that amount in its reserves, it's 100% funded. If it has only $500,000, it's 71% funded. And if it has just $300,000, it's only 43% funded.

This figure matters because it reflects whether the board is properly planning ahead, or kicking the can down the road. While the Davis-Stirling Act doesn't require HOAs to meet any minimum percent funded threshold, the law does require HOAs to levy regular and special assessments that are sufficient to meet its obligations. That means that the percent funded figure gives homeowners one of the clearest and most direct ways to evaluate the relative financial health of their HOA.

Why the "Percent Funded" Number Matters

The "percent funded" figure isn't just a technical calculation. It's one of the fastest ways to assess whether your board is performing one of its most fundamental duties. A healthy reserve "percent funded" figure reflects long-term planning and fiscal responsibility. A weak one suggests poor oversight, deferred maintenance, and quite often a looming special assessment.

This number is required by law. Under the Davis-Stirling Act, every HOA's Assessment and Reserve Funding Disclosure Summary (contained in the annual budget disclosures) must disclose the HOA's current reserve balance, the anticipated cost of repairs, and the "percent funded" figure. It also appears, almost always with more context and detail, in the full reserve study itself. That's important, because while most homeowners never bother reading the full reserve studies (they are dry and complicated), they are more likely to review the annual summary.

In my opinion, if your HOA's "percent funded" figure is in the 70s or higher, that's excellent. A 65% figure is pretty good. A 60% figure is fair. But when the percent funded drops into the 50s, 40s, or lower, that's a red flag, especially if there's no sign that the board plans to raise assessments, cut spending, or revise the reserve strategy. A low "percent funded" figure almost always means that the board is kicking the can down the road and hoping someone else deals with it later. Or even worse, that the board is intentionally manipulating things to artificially (and fraudulently) prop up that figure.[2]

But there's another reason this number matters, and it's often overlooked: reserve obligations are not speculative, they aren't hypothetical, and they aren't contingent on what might happen in a lawsuit or natural disaster. These are repairs and replacements that are going to happen. The roof will wear out. The asphalt will crack. The balconies will need replacing. In fact, the component timelines and cost estimates in reserve studies prepared by qualified professionals are remarkably predictable. Professional reserve specialists calculate useful life and remaining life figures based on decades of performance data and physical inspections supported by tens of thousands of real-life data points.

So when a board underfunds reserves, it's not just underestimating the future. It's actively ignoring it. And the "percent funded" figure gives homeowners a way to see that risk coming. That, of course, presupposes that the figure has been reported honestly and has not been wrongfully manipulated to give a false impression as to the real financial condition of the HOA. If the board is omitting major components, lowballing cost estimates, or fraudulently extending the life of deteriorating assets—all of which artificially prop up the "percent funded" figure—then that figure won't reflect reality.

How Bad HOA Boards Falsify the "Percent Funded" Figure

The "percent funded" figure only means something if it's grounded in honest numbers. When prepared correctly, by a competent and independent reserve analyst, the figure reflects a reality-based snapshot of the HOA's long-term financial position. But when that process is hijacked,

---

2. Some industry standards, such as those published in the National Reserve Study Standards, claim that a 30% or 40% figure is still "adequate." I strongly disagree. In my real-world experience, having dealt with thousands of clients throughout California, a number that low usually reflects years of systemic neglect by badly managed HOAs.

either by board members looking to hide the truth, or by weak professionals willing to compromise under pressure, the figure becomes a smokescreen. And homeowners are left holding the bag (almost always in the form of massive special assessments).

To understand how manipulation of the "percent funded" figure typically happens, it's critical to distinguish between appropriate adjustments made by legitimate professionals and those made (or insisted upon) by fraudulent HOA boards.

Proper Adjustments Made by Qualified Professionals

Not all adjustments to the reserve study figures are improper. On the contrary, competent reserve specialists routinely update component timelines, useful life estimates, and replacement cost projections as part of their ongoing work. These adjustments are based on updated physical inspections, market conditions, inflation, and material performance data.

But it's important to understand that regional factors like salt air, UV exposure, temperature swings, and humidity are already baked into the original estimates. A particular roof located in Palm Springs will not be expected to last the same number of years (i.e., likely won't have the same useful life) as an identical roof located in San Francisco. Those location-based realities are accounted for from the beginning. What prompts a re-evaluation is a deviation from the norm.

For example, if the original study assumed that the area receives an average of six inches of rain per year, and the past year saw less than one inch, those unseasonably dry conditions might lead to reduced wood rot in certain major wood components. In that case, a reserve specialist might lengthen the component's useful life based on observed reduction in the expected deterioration. That's not manipulation. It's responsible, evidence-based planning.

Qualified professionals will document these kinds of adjustments in their reports. They'll explain the cause, justify the change, and base it on what they saw in the field rather than on what the board wants to see or hear. That's what distinguishes professional reserve planning from political gamesmanship and fraud.

Improper Influence and Fraudulent Manipulation

While competent professionals rely on physical inspections and data to make adjustments, bad HOA boards, and sometimes the reserve preparers they pressure, take a different approach. Their goal isn't to plan responsibly. It's to make the HOA's finances appear better than they really are in the present, even if it means putting the community at risk at some vague future date.

It often starts with subtle pressure. A bad HOA board might suggest extending the useful life of a major component by "just a few years" even when there's no evidence to support the change. Or they might push for lower replacement cost estimates, claiming they can probably get a better deal when the time comes. Some boards go further by intentionally removing major components from the reserve schedule entirely (or "delisting" them), or reclassifying them as general maintenance items (referred to as "defunding") to avoid triggering long-term funding obligations.

If the reserve preparer is weak or financially dependent on keeping the board's business, they may go along with it. In those cases, the reserve study becomes less about objective planning and more about presenting a fiction to the HOA members. Sometimes, boards don't even bother with subtlety. They'll override the preparer's conclusions outright, editing the reserve study after it's delivered, refusing access to key areas of the property during inspection, or demanding that certain assumptions be included despite clear evidence to the contrary.

These actions are not just irresponsible. They're fraudulent. A board has no business making unilateral changes to a reserve study. Ever. That is especially true when those changes directly contradict the professional's findings or eliminate core components that will inevitably need repair or replacement in the future. When a board alters a study to inflate the "percent funded" figure, it isn't saving the HOA money. It's setting the HOA and its members up for a future financial crisis.

In one HOA, for example, the board directed the reserve preparer to extend the useful life of three sets of elevated wooden staircases, claiming they looked "fine" and didn't need replacement anytime soon. The preparer, under pressure to keep the board happy, agreed to list their remaining life as 15 years. But during that same year, multiple residents had reported visible dry rot, splintering, and instability in the stairs—all clear signs of deterioration. The board made no effort to inspect or repair the structures. By the time it became impossible for even the board to ignore the deteriorating conditions, there was no money set aside to repair or replace the staircases, and every home-owner ended up having to pay a special assessment of $37,000. The HOA, of course, claimed that the expense had been "unforeseen," but that was completely untrue. The truth was that the special assessment arose directly as a result of years of systemic failure by the board to maintain the stairs, as well as years of blatant fraud in manipulating multiple reserve studies to conceal the true condition of that particular component.

What HOAs Are Legally Allowed (and Not Allowed) to Do With Reserve Funds

Under California law, reserve funds are not just another bank account that the board can dip into at will. The Davis-Stirling Act places strict limitations on how and when reserve funds can be used. These limita-tions exist to ensure that money set aside for major repairs and replace-ments is actually there when it's needed.

Unfortunately, HOAs from Hell either ignore these restrictions or don't understand them. Some treat the reserve account as a slush fund for unrelated expenses. Others "borrow" from reserves without following the required procedures (which include repayment). These are not technical violations. They're serious breaches of fiduciary duty that expose the entire HOA to serious financial risks.

Permitted Use of Reserve Funds

Civil Code section 5510 clearly and concisely establishes how reserve funds may be spent:

- The repair or replacement of the major components that the HOA is obligated to maintain, as identified in the most recent reserve study.

- Litigation involving the repair or replacement of those same components.

That's it. Routine operating expenses, landscaping contracts, management company bonuses, or unexpected legal fees unrelated to capital components cannot be paid from the reserve account.

Reserve funds are not meant to make the board's life easier in the short term. They exist to protect the long-term stability of the community. In other words, they exist to ensure that when a $400,000 roof replacement comes due, there's money in the bank to cover it.

Borrowing From Reserves: What the Law Allows and What the Law Doesn't Allow

Civil Code section 5515 does allow boards to temporarily borrow from reserves when the need arises, but only under strict conditions. If the board chooses to borrow reserve funds for other purposes, it must:

- Place the item on the agenda of an open board meeting and notify the members of its intent to borrow.

- Explain the reason for the transfer, propose options for repayment, and disclose whether a special assessment may be needed to restore (i.e., repay) the funds.

- Once the transfer is approved, record in the meeting minutes the justification for the borrowing and the repayment plan.

- Repay the money to the reserve account within one year unless the board documents in writing why a longer period is in the best interest of the association.

These rules aren't optional. They're mandatory. And they're designed to ensure transparency, accountability, and responsible reserve management.

How to Spot, and Respond to, Misuse of Reserve Funds

Boards that misuse reserve funds rarely leave an obvious smoking gun. But they do leave patterns, such as paper trails, omissions, and inconsistencies that don't add up. And if you know what to look for, you can spot the signs before the damage grows too large.

Below are some of the clearest red flags that your board may be misusing, misreporting, or illegally borrowing from the HOA's reserves:

- **Major components are missing (periodically or otherwise) from the reserve study**. If the development has wooden staircases, balconies, retaining walls, or flat roofs that obviously need upkeep, but none of those components appear in the reserve schedule, then that's a good indication that something is wrong.

- **Remaining life figures that don't match visible reality**. If a deck is visibly cracked, rotting, or unsafe, but the reserve study says it has 15 years left on its useful life, that's not just a mistake. It's a red flag that someone is manipulating the data. And by looking at prior reserve studies (or summaries) to compare, you can often determine when the wrongdoing started.

- **Replacement cost estimates that are wildly off.** If the reserve study lists a $400,000 roof replacement at $190,000, or if other numbers seem suspiciously low based on local market conditions, that's a sign the board or preparer is lowballing to inflate the "percent funded" figure.

- **Identical components listed with different lifespans.** If two buildings in the same development have the same type of balconies, built at the same time with the same materials, but the study lists them as having 12 years and 20 years remaining, that's a serious inconsistency. Unless there's a clear explanation set forth in an applicable reserve study, you should consider that a serious red flag.

- **No reserve study updates or revisions after visible deterioration.** If obvious damage or aging has occurred, like cracked concrete, rusted railings, or water intrusion, but the reserve study hasn't been updated or adjusted, that's a sign the board is ignoring new evidence or shielding the truth.

- **Sudden drops in reserve balance without a known repair project.** This may signal that funds were transferred without disclosure or used for improper purposes.

- **No board discussion of a repayment plan after a reserve transfer.** If the HOA admits to "borrowing" from reserves, but there's no documentation of how and when the money will be repaid, that's a statutory violation under Civil Code section 5515.

- **Vague or missing meeting minutes.** If financial transfers or project decisions don't appear in the board's meeting records, or appear as ambiguous references, that's a classic tactic to avoid scrutiny.

- **The board claims a major expense was "unforeseen."** If homeowners are suddenly hit with a huge special assessment for something predictable, such as a roof, deck, or stair replacement, that's often a cover story for reserve mismanagement or fraud.

If you suspect something isn't right, here's what you can do:

- **Request financial records.** As we discussed in Chapter 4, under Civil Code section 5200, HOA members have a legal right to inspect a remarkably large list of HOA-related documents that will show you where reserve money has gone.

- **Demand board meeting minutes from the past 12–18 months.** If the board borrowed from reserves, there must be a recorded vote, a documented reason for the transfer, and a repayment plan. If those minutes don't exist, or if the board claims the decision wasn't discussed publicly, then they've violated Civil Code section 5515.

- **Ask the tough questions on the record.** At the next open meeting, challenge the board directly: When was the money transferred? Where is the repayment plan? Why wasn't the membership notified? Boards that are hiding something will often deflect or delay. But if you raise the issue clearly, and on the record, you've already changed the power dynamic. Demand that your questions (and the board's answers or non-responses) be reflected in the minutes. Then follow up after the minutes come out. If the details you demanded are not reflected in the minutes, send an email pointing that fact out and detailing the missing facts.

- **Demand that the issue be added to the next board meeting agenda.** Don't just raise the issue during general comments. Ask, in writing, that the board place the item on the next meeting agenda as a scheduled business item. That forces the board to acknowledge it publicly. And if they refuse, it helps build your case for enforcement or legal action. Be sure to document their refusal in writing.

- **Rally other homeowners.** Boards are far more likely to back down, or correct course, when they realize you're not the only one paying attention. Share what you've found with neighbors. Organize a group demand letter. Use numbers to build pressure.

Misuse of reserve funds isn't just a technical violation. It's a serious breach of trust that can cost homeowners tens of thousands of dollars. The law gives you the right to uncover it, challenge it, and stop it. But that only works if you're willing to speak up and take action.

Legal Enforcement: What Happens If Your HOA Ignores Your Demand

Most homeowners assume that if their HOA violates the law, some agency or government office will step in to investigate and set things right. That's not how it works in California. The Davis-Stirling Act imposes strict legal obligations on HOA boards relating to financial disclosures, reserve account management, transparency, and document access, but it offers no state enforcement mechanism. There's no regulator, no oversight body, and no one from Sacramento who's going to show up and hold your board accountable.

If the law is going to be enforced, it has to be enforced by you.

Start with a Demand

Before pursuing legal action, it's always smart to send a formal written demand. This isn't about giving the board a free pass. *It's about documenting the violation, creating a paper trail* (and, of course, giving them one final opportunity to comply). That demand should be clear, specific, and cite the statutes the board is violating. For example:

- If the board failed to include a "percent funded" figure or reserve disclosures in the annual budget report, cite Civil Code sections 5300 and 5570 and demand the board's compliance.

- If your board "borrowed" from reserves without meeting the notice, documentation, and repayment plan requirements, cite section 5515, and demand the board's compliance.

- If your board refuses to produce the documents you requested, such as the meeting minutes, financial records, or the reserve study itself, cite section 5200, and again, demand the board's compliance.

Give the board a firm deadline to comply. Keep a copy of your letter and proof of delivery. This step is not only practical, but it significantly strengthens your legal position if and when you decide to escalate.

What if Your HOA Ignores You

If the board refuses to comply after you've issued a formal written demand, then it's time to consider legal action. That may involve filing a petition to compel compliance, initiating a lawsuit, or in some cases first offering ADR.

Under Civil Code section 5930, certain types of HOA disputes require homeowners to offer ADR before suing. But that rule doesn't apply to everything. For example, petitions to compel record production under section 5235 may not trigger the ADR requirements. Nor would an action to enforce basic financial disclosures.

Regardless, if litigation becomes necessary, your specific legal claims will depend on the facts. Common causes of action include breach of fiduciary duty, negligence, breach of contract (i.e., breach of the governing documents), and other Davis-Stirling Act violations. This is when you need to speak with an attorney who actually understands HOA law, not just real estate law or contracts in general. A qualified HOA attorney can help you determine which causes of action apply, how to structure your case, and whether you'll be entitled to recover attorneys' fees and costs if you prevail, which, in most cases like these, you will.

If your HOA refuses to follow the law, you don't have to tolerate it. You just have to be ready to act because when boards aren't held accountable, homeowners are the ones who pay the price.

Balcony Inspections and the Davis-Stirling Act

In the wake of some high profile balcony collapses in California, the Legislature passed what is known as California's "Balcony Law." The Balcony Law consists of a set of regulations designed to enhance the safety of exterior elevated elements ("EEEs") in multi-unit dwellings of three or more homes. As codified in the Davis-Stirling Act as Civil Code sections 5551 and 5986, the Balcony Law mandates a two-pronged approach to exterior elevated elements ("EEE") safety: (i) mandatory inspections; and (ii) repair and replacement.

In short, the law requires visual inspections (or if necessary, invasive testing) of load-bearing components and associated waterproofing systems of any EEEs (e.g., balconies, decks, porches, stairways, walkways, or their railings) made of or supported by wood at least once every nine years. The inspections focus on evaluating the integrity and safety of load-bearing components, identifying any signs of deterioration such as dry rot, termite damage, or water intrusion that could compromise structural integrity.

The Legislature imposed the nine-year interval in an attempt to balance the need for regular oversight with the logistical and financial burden placed on HOAs. While the nine-year frequency aims to identify deterioration early (i.e., before a problem escalates into a safety hazard), if an inspection reveals damage or deterioration that poses an immediate safety threat, HOAs are required to make immediate repairs/replacements. For less urgent repairs, however, HOAs are permitted to prepare their own timelines/budgets for completing the work while taking into account the relative severity of the issues and their respective HOA's financial resources.

To help ensure a necessary level of expertise, the Balcony Law requires that the inspections be conducted by licensed architects, civil/structural engineers, or certified building inspectors. The inspection's scope includes evaluating visible and accessible elements, as well as conducting probing and testing where necessary. Inspectors must document their findings comprehensively, and once the inspector has completed the inspection, he or she must provide the HOA with a detailed written report: (i) identifying the components/systems tested; (ii) identifying the condition of the association's EEEs, including any safety concerns; (iii) indicating the expected future performance/remaining life of the load-bearing components and associated waterproofing systems; and (iv) recommending necessary repairs and/or replacements of those items. (Civ. Code, § 5551(e).)

While HOAs in California were required to complete their initial inspections no later than January 1, 2025, with subsequent inspections required every nine years, many have not done so, leaving a good number of HOAs in potentially severe legal and financial jeopardy.[3]

The Balcony Law's requirements do not just present as a safety requirement. They are a budgeting requirement too—one with major financial consequences for HOAs and their members. Balcony repairs, especially when structural elements are compromised, can run into the hundreds of thousands, if not millions, of dollars for large communities. The law does not give associations an "out" because they failed to budget for these repairs in advance. That means the only fiscally responsible way to comply with the Balcony Law is to account for the inspections and any necessary repairs in the HOA's reserve study and long-term maintenance plan.

And yet, thousands of boards across thousands of HOAs in California have completely dropped the ball in this regard. This is precisely the

---

3. For buildings constructed after January 1, 2020, the initial inspection must occur within six years of issuance of the certificate of occupancy.

reason why my law firm has seen so many massive special assessments (e.g., special assessments totaling more than $25,000 per household) passed in thousands of HOAs throughout the State of California since the law's enactment.

Such failures on the part of fiscally unsound HOA boards are inconsistent with their fiduciary duties and the reserve study requirements under the Davis-Stirling Act. Civil Code section 5551 is not optional, and failing to plan for it in the reserve study is a red flag for poor financial management, or worse, intentional manipulation to justify bypassing member approval for large assessments later.

For homeowners, the takeaway is simple: check your HOA's most recent reserve study and budget. Look for a line item covering both the cost of the inspection and projected repair costs for balconies, decks, and other exterior elevated elements. If it's missing, ask the board why, and get their response in writing. If the reserve study fails to include these costs, the board is effectively guaranteeing a future "emergency" special assessment when the inspection report inevitably uncovers years of systemic deterioration.

Emergency Special Assessments

Under California law, boards generally cannot impose a special assessment that exceeds 5% of the HOA's annual budgeted gross expenses without first getting membership approval. Civil Code section 5610, however, creates a narrow "emergency" exception to that rule. This is the same exception some boards will claim applies to Balcony Law repairs when reserves are inadequate.

If the board imposes a special assessment under the emergency exception, it still has a legal duty to notify all members. Civil Code section 5615 requires that written notice of the assessment be delivered to each member between 30 and 60 days before the assessment becomes due. That notice must include:

- The total amount of the assessment.

- The reason it is being levied (including the nature of the emergency).

- The due date(s) and payment schedule.

This requirement is not optional. Even when there is a valid emergency, failing to give the proper written notice is a violation of the Davis-Stirling Act.

ANNUAL BUDGET RELATED DISCLOSURES	
Specific Disclosure	Civ. Code Section
A pro forma operating budget, showing the estimated revenue and expenses on an accrual basis	§ 5300(b)(1)
Summary of HOA reserves	§§ 5300(b)(2) and 5565
Summary of reserve funding plan	§§ 5300(b)(3) and 5550(b)(5)
A statement as to whether the board has determined to defer or not undertake repairs or replacement of any major component and justification for the decision	§ 5300(b)(4)
A statement about any anticipated special assessments	§ 5300(b)(5)
A statement about how the board will fund reserves to repair or replace major components (e.g., assessments, loans, deferrals of selected repairs, etc.)	§ 5300(b)(6)
A statement outlining the procedures used to calculate reserves	§§ 5300(b)(7) and 5570(b)(4)
A statement as to whether the association has any outstanding loans and the payment terms (e.g., interest rate being charged, amount outstanding, etc.)	§ 5300(b)(8)
A summary of the HOA's applicable insurance policies (e.g., liability, earthquake, flood, etc.), along with the name of the insurer, policy limits, deductibles, etc.	§ 5300(b)(9)
For condominium owners, a statement describing whether the development is an FHA-approved condominium project*	§ 5300(b)(10)
For condominium owners, a statement describing whether the development is a VA-approved condominium project**	§ 5300(b)(11)
A disclosure of the document fees charged to potential purchasers	§§ 5300(b)(12) and 4528

An Assessment and Reserve Funding Disclosure Summary form	§§ 5300(e) and 5570

* This is important because buyers who purchase condominiums in non-FHA-approved developments will not be able to obtain FHA-backed loans (which accounts for most home loans).

**This is important because unless an HOA is approved by the VA, eligible veterans and active duty members of the military will not be able to purchase condominiums using VA loans (or take advantage of the benefits of VA loans, such as no down payment, no private mortgage insurance, etc.).

ANNUAL POLICY-RELATED DISCLOSURES	
Specific Disclosure	Civ. Code Section
Name and address of the person designated by the HOA to receive official communications on the HOA's behalf	Civ. Code, §§ 5310(a)(1) and 4035
A statement explaining that a member may submit a request to have notices sent to up to two different specified addresses	Civ. Code, §§ 5310(a)(2) and 4040(b)
Notice of the location designated for the posting of general notices (e.g., agendas for meetings, etc.)	Civ. Code, §§ 5310(a)(3) and 4045(a)
Notice of your right to receive general notices by individual delivery	§§ 5310(a)(4) and 4045(b)
Notice of your right to receive minutes of the open board meetings (not executive session)	§§ 5310(a)(5) and 4950(b)
A statement regarding the HOA's assessment collection policies	§§ 5310(a)(6) and 5730
A statement regarding the HOA's default and enforcement policies (including enforcement via liens)	§ 5310(a)(7)
A statement regarding the HOA's discipline policies, and where applicable, its fine schedule	§§ 5310(a)(8) and 5850
A summary of the HOA's dispute resolution procedures (e.g., ADR)	§§ 5310(a)(9), 5920, and 5965
A summary of any applicable architectural guidelines	§§ 5310(a)(10) and 4765(c)
Mailing address for overnight payment of assessments	§§ 5310(a)(11) and 5655
Property manager certification disclosures	Bus. & Prof. Code, § 5310(a)(1)

MEMBER DISCIPLINE
AND DUE PROCESS

WHEN AN HOA wants to discipline a homeowner for violating a rule, failing to pay money owed to the HOA, or damaging the common area, it has to follow a series of steps before it can impose punishment. That includes sending written notice of a hearing, giving the homeowner a chance to be heard, and formally voting on the discipline in a closed session. These requirements exist for a reason: to protect homeowners from retaliation, abuse, and selective enforcement, and to provide homeowners with due process.

But in practice, bad HOA boards (and a lot of them are bad) treat these steps like a formality. They give vague notices, conduct rubber-stamp hearings, and use the process not to evaluate the facts, but to justify a decision they've already made. Some boards even use the hearing process as a means of retaliation, targeting homeowners whom they don't like for personal reasons, or who ask tough questions or challenge board authority. And thanks to a new law called AB 130, a process that was at least pretty clear in how things were supposed to work has been turned on its head.

This chapter walks through the discipline process under Civil Code sections 5850–5855. It explains what counts as a valid notice, what rights you have at the hearing, and when the board's actions cross the line. It also unpacks the procedural changes made by AB 130, including new limits on fines, new enforcement mechanisms, and new risks that most homeowners and attorneys are completely unaware of. If your board is using discipline to intimidate or silence you, this chapter will help you push back.

Discipline: What HOAs Are Permitted To Do to Their Members

One of the most fundamental duties of an HOA is to enforce the governing documents, and the Davis-Stirling Act explicitly requires HOA boards to do just that. In accomplishing that fundamental task, HOA boards must always act strictly within the scope and limits of their authority and follow all required due process-related procedures.

In other words, boards can only discipline homeowners in ways that the law allows. And when they cross the line by, for example, punishing people without proper authority or enforcing rules that don't hold legal weight, their actions become illegal.

This segment breaks down what disciplinary tools HOA boards are allowed to use, what limits the law places on them, and how those powers differ depending on the type of violation and the structure of the community.

What "Discipline" Actually Means in the HOA Context

Within the meaning of the Davis-Stirling Act, "Discipline" includes a wide range of consequences that an HOA board can impose for rule violations. Common forms of member discipline include:

- Providing written warnings.

- Imposing monetary penalties (i.e., fines).

- Suspending common area privileges (e.g., pool, gym, clubhouse).

- Suspending the right to certain privileges (e.g., valet, package delivery, guest check-in).

- Temporary removal from committees or volunteer roles.

These disciplinary actions must be tied to a violation of the governing documents. Boards cannot impose discipline based on arbitrary or capricious standards, personal preferences, or unwritten expectations. And discipline isn't valid just because the board wants it to be. If the authority to impose a specific penalty doesn't exist—i.e., it's not grounded in a specific statute or provision of a governing document—or if the board fails to follow the proper procedures, then the punishment will be deemed unlawful and unenforceable.

On June 30, 2025, AB 130 went into effect. That new law capped HOA fines at $100 per violation, unless the violation involves a "significant and imminent threat to health or safety." It also banned late fees and interest charges on unpaid fines, reduced the board's post-hearing notice window from 15 to 14 days, and added vague new procedures that disrupted long-standing enforcement norms. While the fine cap at least stops one form of overreach, many experts, including myself, believe that it will create far more problems than it solved. This book will dive deeper into some of the problems with AB 130 later in this chapter.

Fines Require a Published Fine Schedule

Before a board can impose any monetary penalty on a homeowner, the HOA must have a properly adopted and disclosed fine schedule. This is not a technicality. It's a legal requirement under Civil Code section 5850, and it is reinforced by Civil Code section 5310(a)(8), which mandates that the association's disciplinary policy and fine schedule be distributed annually as part of the HOA's annual policy statement.

The fine schedule doesn't need to list every individual rule, but it must describe the categories of violations for which fines may be imposed, along with the corresponding dollar amounts. If a fine is not clearly authorized by the published schedule, it may be invalid. HOAs that skip this step, or fail to update and circulate the fine schedule each year, may lose the legal authority to impose fines altogether. Courts have held that fines must be based on rules that were validly adopted, properly disclosed, and reasonably applied. Anything less opens the board's use of fines as a means of discipline to legal challenge.

Case Study

A client of ours originally came to us for help in a dispute over his architectural plans. During the course of our representation, we discovered that the board had been fining him repeatedly for parking violations that occurred while his construction project was underway. With contractors and equipment on-site, he had no reasonable options for parking. We were prepared to argue that fining him under those circumstances was unfair and unreasonable.

But when we dug deeper, we found something even more powerful. Civil Code section 5850 requires every HOA to adopt and distribute a written schedule of fines before imposing them. When we demanded proof, the HOA couldn't produce one. They had never adopted a fine schedule.

That discovery changed everything. No matter how strongly the board felt about its parking rules, without a published fine schedule, every penalty they imposed was unenforceable. We notified the HOA that if it didn't rescind the fines, it faced a lawsuit it couldn't win and attorney's fees it would end up paying.

The board backed down, and reimbursed our client for all of the fines he'd paid. Our client didn't just avoid hundreds of dollars in penalties, but he avoided escalating enforcement with no immediate end in sight. This is the power of due process. Even when you think you've broken a rule, the board must follow the law. When it doesn't, you hold the leverage.

The Purpose of Fines Matters

Most HOAs' CC&Rs empower their HOAs to fine members who violate the rules. The Davis-Stirling Act authorizes boards to exercise such power solely to deter rule violations. The power to fine, however, is not intended to serve as a revenue source for the HOA, and thus boards cannot use them to balance the budget, pad the reserves, or punish people out of frustration or retaliation. The goal is, and always has been, behavioral compliance. When boards lose sight of that, the entire enforcement process becomes tainted and deeply problematic. *Fairminded HOA members understand the purpose and need for just penalties for infractions (a law with no teeth might as well not exist). They don't understand, nor should they tolerate, penalties designed to raise revenue.*

Even when a fine is technically authorized, the board must still act reasonably. Courts don't require a formal showing that a fine was meant to deter. But in the hands of a competent HOA attorney, they will look at whether the enforcement approach feels retaliatory, inconsistent, or grossly disproportionate to the offense. If a board uses fines to intimidate, to retaliate, or primarily to generate revenue, that fine becomes vulnerable to legal challenge.

Before AB 130 went into effect, some HOAs exploited this area of discretion. In one of my podcast episodes, I discussed a situation that occurred in a Northern California HOA.[1] In that example, I discussed how an HOA up north issued multiple $175 fines for minor parking violations after having installed surveillance cameras all over the community with the primary intention of raising funds for the HOA. Some owners were fined thousands of dollars in just a few months. And the board raked in tens of thousands more.

The bottom line is that deterrence must be the goal, not dollars.

---

1. You can find my podcast, HOA HELL, on several of the major podcast platforms, and on YouTube at https://www.youtube.com/@HOAHELLpodcastofficial.

Limits on Suspension of Privileges

HOA discipline isn't limited to fines. HOAs can also suspend privileges when a member violates the governing documents. But like fines, such discipline has its limits. For example, while certain types of suspensions are permissible, others are always illegal.

For obvious reasons, suspension of privileges as a meaningful form of member discipline really only comes into play in associations with multiple types of member amenities, including things like:

- Access to recreational amenities like pools, gyms, and tennis courts.

- Use of clubhouses or meeting facilities (except during election events).

- Participation in committees or volunteer roles.

- Manned security gates.

- Valet parking, concierge services, guest check-in, and package delivery.

- Guest parking in communities with assigned or monitored spaces.

If the governing documents allow it, and due process is followed, boards may suspend those types of non-essential privileges.[2]

By contrast, boards cannot, under any circumstances, suspend essential rights or services, involving any of the following:

- **Ingress and egress.** Owners and residents always have the right to enter and exit their homes.

---

2. Boards may also suspend a tenant's privileges if the property owner becomes delinquent or violates the governing documents. That's because the owner typically transfers those rights to the tenant through the lease. Once the owner loses those rights, the tenant loses them too.

- **Essential Utilities and elevator access**. HOAs cannot suspend essential services, such as water, electricity, gas, trash collection, or elevator use because those are considered necessary for habitability. HOAs may, however, suspend certain non-essential services (like cable, satellite, intercom, or internet) if those services are provided through a bulk contract and the governing documents allow it.

- **Voting rights**. Boards may not suspend a member's right to vote in board elections.

- **Meeting attendance**. All members may attend open board meetings, regardless of their status.

- **Access to election facilities**. HOAs cannot restrict member access to meeting rooms or polling spaces used for elections, including a clubhouse that the member is otherwise prohibited from using.

Any board that tries to suspend those rights is breaking the law.

Special Consideration for Tenants and Trusts

Not every property is occupied by its legal owner. In many HOAs, units are leased to tenants or held in family trusts for estate planning purposes. That doesn't exempt those properties from discipline, but it does affect how the HOA can enforce its rules.

When a homeowner rents out their unit, the tenant typically inherits the owner's right to use the common areas. But that also means the tenant is subject to the same rules, and the board can respond to violations just as it would with an owner. If the governing documents allow it, the HOA can suspend a tenant's privileges when the owner is delinquent or under disciplinary suspension. That includes access to recreational areas, guest parking, or concierge services. The board doesn't need to discipline the tenant directly. It only needs to act on the owner's rights, which the tenant loses by extension.

This enforcement method is especially important in high-density communities, where absentee landlords may ignore problems caused by their tenants unless there's a consequence that affects them directly.

Trust-held properties raise a different issue. A trust is not a legal person, like a corporation or a limited liability company. Trusts are considered "testamentary vehicles," intended to hold assets (like a house) so they can be managed during your lifetime and then passed to your heirs when you die. The HOA cannot impose fines or discipline against a trust itself. But the trustee, the individual named on the deed, can be disciplined if the property's residents violate the governing documents. When problems arise, the HOA must direct enforcement to the trustee by name, and not, say, to "The Smith Family Trust" or any other non-entity. That preserves the legal chain of responsibility and ensures that any penalties are properly issued.

Due Process: HOAs Must Follow Certain Procedures Before Disciplining Members

Boards don't get to discipline members in any manner that they may want to. The Davis-Stirling Act doesn't just authorize enforcement, it limits it. And before a board can fine a member, suspend privileges, or take other disciplinary action, it must follow a very specific legal process.

That process is called "due process," and it exists for a reason.

Due process protects homeowners from retaliatory, selective, and arbitrary discipline. It forces the board to slow down, follow the rules, and give the member a real opportunity to respond and be heard. And when the board fails to follow it, the penalties they impose become legally vulnerable, regardless of how "clear" the violation might seem.

Procedural v. Substantive Due Process

When most people hear the term "due process," they think only of procedure. And it's true. *Procedural due process* is a critical part of due process. Procedural due process requires fair notice, a hearing, and a written decision. Without those steps, disciplinary action is unenforceable no matter how obvious the violation might seem.

But due process also has a second dimension. Substance. *Substantive due process* requires that a board's decision itself be reasonable, i.e., that their decision *not* be arbitrary, capricious, or retaliatory. Even if the hearing process is flawless, a punishment that is clearly disproportionate, unsupported by the governing documents, or applied selectively, will not withstand legal scrutiny.

One practical example of how the two work together involves anonymous complaints. Disciplinary hearings cannot be based solely on anonymous testimony because that deprives the accused homeowner of the ability to confront or challenge the evidence. That would constitute a failure of *procedural due process*. And any penalty issued on nothing more than an anonymous statement would also be arbitrary and unreasonable, violating the principle of *substantive due process*. But if the violation is independently verified through reliable evidence, such as security camera recordings or board member observations, the hearing may proceed without disclosing the complaining neighbor's identity. Courts have upheld the use of corroborated evidence without requiring the direct appearance of witnesses, provided that the evidence is reliable and sufficient to support the findings. This strikes the balance that California law requires between protecting fairness for the accused and allowing enforcement when credible, corroborated evidence exists.

The distinction between procedural and substantive due process matters because it gives homeowners two lines of defense. If the board fails to follow the proper procedures, the penalty is invalid on procedural grounds. And even if the procedures are properly followed, the penalty can still be attacked substantively if it lacks fairness or consistency.

In short, *procedural due process* governs the process or procedure in which a decision is made, while *substantive due process* governs how the decision is reached. Both are required under California law, and a failure in either category renders the discipline legally vulnerable.

What Civil Code § 5855 Required Before AB 130 Changed Things

Civil Code section 5855 spells out the minimum procedural steps a board must take before imposing any form of discipline on a member. And until June 30, 2025, those steps were relatively straightforward, requiring the following:

- **Advance written notice of the alleged violation.** The board had to notify the member in writing at least 10 days before the hearing. That notice needed to include the date, time, and location of the hearing, a description of the alleged violation, and a statement that the member had the right to attend and be heard. Delivery had to be by personal service or by mail (or by electronic means if the member consented in writing).

- **A private hearing before the board.** The hearing had to be held in executive session, meaning that the proceedings would not be open to other members, and the homeowner had to be allowed to attend and respond. The board couldn't hold a public trial or deny the member an opportunity to speak.

- **A written decision delivered within 15 days of the hearing.** The board had to deliver its written decision within 15 calendar days of the hearing. That deadline applied to all forms of discipline, including fines and suspension of privileges.

Those were the due process requirements that applied to every HOA disciplinary action in California before June 30, 2025. They formed the basic framework: notice, hearing, and decision. The process was simple and straightforward. Later in this chapter, we'll examine how AB 130 upended the disciplinary process and made some important parts of the process hopelessly vague and problematic. In the next section, however, we look at what happens when boards skip these requirements (or pretend to follow them without actually doing so).

When Boards Ignore Due Process, or Fake It

Most bad HOA boards don't come out and say they're ignoring the law. Instead, they stage just enough of a "process" to make it look like they've followed the rules even when they haven't.

Sometimes the board never holds a hearing at all, although that's happening much less frequently. More often, the hearing notice is so vague that the homeowner has no idea what they're being accused of, or the hearing is scheduled, but it's obvious from the beginning that the board has already made its decision behind closed doors. This, of course, transforms what should've been a fair proceeding into a fruitless formality.

That's not legal.

Discipline that doesn't strictly follow the minimum requirements of Civil Code section 5855 is unenforceable. That includes improperly noticed hearings, missing decision letters, and skipped procedural steps. When a board fakes the process, it loses the legal protection that would normally shield its actions from challenge.[3]

---

3. AB 130, which went into effect on June 30, 2025, include several new provisions that directly affect member due process, such as the right to avoid a hearing by showing a "financial commitment," mandatory IDR, and enforceable hearing outcomes. Those changes are addressed separately later in this chapter. The due process steps listed above reflect the law before those changes took effect.

AB 130: How California's New $100 Fine Cap Changed the Rules

As of June 30, 2025, California HOAs can no longer impose monetary fines greater than "$100 per violation," unless the violation involves a "significant and imminent threat to health or safety." This new cap, part of AB 130,[4] was inserted into a few different sections of the Davis-Stirling Act (e.g., Civil Code §§ 5850 and 5855) with little fanfare and even less clarity. And while AB 130 appears at first blush to be a welcome protection against abusive boards, the truth is far more complicated.

On its surface, AB 130 looks like a win for homeowners. Thus far, it has even fooled a lot of so-called expert homeowner-side attorneys who ought to know better. The truth is that AB 130 is unforgivably vague and is already causing more problems than it could've ever hoped to solve. It says nothing about escalating fines or the legality of daily penalties for ignored violations. It also says nothing about the previously frowned upon practice of "stacking" that bad HOAs used to rely on (and which good HOAs will probably now have to implement just to prevent people from ignoring penalties as the cost of doing business).[5]

That silence leaves every board, every manager, and every homeowner in the position of having to guess what's allowed. We've been left with

---

4. The one exception to the $100 cap involves violations that present a "significant and imminent threat to health or safety." But again, the law gives no guidance as to what qualifies. Yes, the statute puts the decision as to what qualifies into the hands of the HOA board, but with no definitional guidance from the Legislature, different judges in different courts will have different opinions, and HOA boards could face massive attorneys' fees awards against them if they don't choose wisely.

5. Stacking refers to the practice of an HOA board issuing multiple violation letters or notices for the same continuing offense in order to multiply fines or penalties. It's frowned upon because Civil Code § 5855 requires that each fine follow proper notice and hearing procedures. In the past, stacking letters to inflate enforcement undermined due process and exposed the HOA to claims of abuse and selective enforcement. After AB 130, however, it might become a reasonable way for HOAs to navigate the new law.

some extremely blurred lines, and in such cases, the bad HOAs will continue to do whatever they want until a court slaps them down, and the good HOAs will be more cautious by not acting. So the only winners will be the bad HOAs and the bad HOA members (those who violate the rules to benefit themselves at the expense of their fellow members). In other words, the good HOAs will under-enforce to avoid legal exposure and abuse, and the bad HOAs will do what they always do—overreach and assume that they can do what they want until a court tells them no.

Are Escalating or Daily Fines Still Legal?

AB 130 doesn't just cap fines. It creates a wide gap between what the law says and what boards actually need to know to effectively enforce the rules. And nowhere is that gap more dangerous than when it comes to repeated or ongoing violations.

Under Civil Code section 5850, as amended by AB 130, fines are now capped at $100 "per violation." But the statute never says:

- Whether a board can issue escalating fines for repeat conduct.

- Whether a continuing violation, like a car left parked improperly for ten days, qualifies as one violation or ten.

- Whether a board will have to resort to "stacking" hearing letters just to provide a real disincentive to continue violating.

Before AB 130, most HOA fine schedules included escalating and daily penalties. The first violation might result in a warning. The second, a $50 fine. The third, a $100 fine. And so on. The longer a member continued to violate (or never remedy) a violation, the higher the fine for the same and future violations would be. These schedules gave homeowners a chance to comply before facing steeper consequences, and they gave good HOA boards a tool to deter serial rulebreakers without having to go to court.

Likewise, the same appears to be true for per-day fines. Many HOAs used to impose daily penalties for continuing violations—$25 per day until the homeowner removed the trash, reversed the architectural change, or resolved the nuisance. But AB 130 offers no guidance. If a fine is limited to $100 "per violation," does that mean $100 total for an uncorrected issue no matter how long it persists? Or can the board re-fine each day (following a hearing), treating the same infraction as multiple violations?

That model may now be dead, thus rendering toothless the ability of many HOAs to abide by one of their fundamental duties: enforcing the governing documents.

And that ambiguity rewards the very people this law was never meant to protect—*bad homeowners and bad neighbors*. Most communities have these people, bad neighbors who regularly flout the rules, ignore notices, and disrupt the lives of their neighbors. And now those individuals have every reason to continue flouting the rules regardless of who it hurts. With no clarity on escalating fines, and no ability to impose meaningful daily penalties, good HOA boards have lost one of their only tools to compel compliance without having to go to court.

The $100 cap becomes a price tag. If someone wants to leave construction debris in their yard for weeks, or illegally park a vehicle in a shared driveway every night, they can just write it off as a minor cost—the HOA's version of a parking meter. And for boards that actually care about their communities, that creates a no-win scenario: either spend thousands on litigation to stop a rulebreaker, or let violations slide and undermine the rules entirely. And who's left having to deal with the consequences? The good HOA members who've done nothing wrong. AB 130 didn't just create a policy problem. *It created a neighborhood problem.*

The "Financial Commitment" Loophole

AB 130 added new language to Civil Code section 5855 that lets home-owners avoid a disciplinary hearing altogether by either curing the violation or by showing, prior to the scheduled hearing date, that they made a "financial commitment" to cure the violation.

Huh? I've been an attorney for almost 30 years, and spent many years as a trial attorney. I am considered an expert in HOA law. And I have no idea what that means.

The statute doesn't define what counts as a "financial commitment." It doesn't say whether that means a signed service contract with a contractor or vendor, a mere quote from a contractor or vendor, a down payment made to a contractor or vendor, or simply a promise to act to resolve the infraction (e.g., "I now give you my 'financial commitment' to resolve this"). It doesn't define anything. That lack of clarity isn't just inconvenient. It creates an enforcement loophole that bad homeowners will absolutely exploit.

For example:

- A homeowner cited for a landscaping violation submits a vague invoice showing that they "intend" to have the work completed. Is that enough? The invoice doesn't say when the work will be done. Is that a problem? The statute doesn't say.

- A member facing a hearing for unpermitted construction could flash a contractor quote with no payment attached, just to post-pone enforcement. Would that do it? Who knows?

Meanwhile, the board *appears to now be required to cancel the hearing* upon receipt of such a "financial commitment" even if it suspects the commitment is meaningless.[6] The statute doesn't allow the board to

---

6. That raises another potential problem: the statute is silent as to what's supposed to occur once the board receives such a "financial commitment." Is the disciplinary hearing cancelled? Or does the homeowners still have to show up? And if so, to what end? I don't know. Do you?

proceed and consider whether the cure is legitimate. It forces cancellation with no mechanism for judgment or verification. Or does it? I don't know. Do you?

This provision also complicates timing and procedural flow. If a member sends in a document claiming to satisfy the "financial commitment" requirement, and the board disagrees, what happens? Does the board reschedule the hearing? Restart the 10-day notice period? There's no guidance, just a procedural landmine waiting to be triggered.

Like so many parts of AB 130, this section wasn't designed with real enforcement in mind. It looks like a safeguard, but in practice, it's another untested, undefined, and unworkable rule that benefits bad actors and leaves good boards, as well as good homeowners, stuck cleaning up the mess.

The IDR Problem: Another AB 130 Addition That Creates More Confusion Than Clarity

Before AB 130, Civil Code section 5855 didn't mention IDR at all. Homeowners have always had a right to demand IDR, and HOA boards have always been required to participate upon a homeowner's demand. AB 130 inserted new language into Civil Code section 5855 stating that if the board and the member do not reach agreement at the hearing, the member shall have the opportunity to request IDR under Civil Code section 5910. What's the harm in that?

That depends. If the new language means nothing more than a simple reiteration of a right that homeowners already had, then there's no harm in that particular addition. But what happens if the IDR addition to Civil Code section 5855 is intended to allow the homeowner to reargue (as a sort of appeal) the disciplinary issue by requesting IDR afterward? And does the board have to suspend enforcement until IDR is resolved? What happens if the homeowner sends an IDR demand but doesn't follow through? None of that is clear.

This isn't clarity. It's legislative noise. And like so much of AB 130, it complicates enforcement without offering any real benefit to the people it claims to protect.

AB 130 Turned Hearing Agreements Into Enforceable Judgments

For many years, most HOA disciplinary hearings ended the same way. The board thanked the homeowner for attending, ended the hearing, then deliberated privately in executive session. Later, the board would notify the homeowner of its decision in writing within the prior 15-day timeframe.

AB 130 may have changed that. Civil Code section 5855(e) now says that if the board and the homeowner reach an agreement during the hearing, the board must draft a written resolution. If both sides sign it, the agreement becomes judicially enforceable.

That sounds simple, but it's not.

This new requirement, consisting of just two short sentences, says nothing about some pretty important issues, including:

- **How wide in scope the "agreement" should or can be**. Remember, the homeowner is at the hearing because the member has been accused of violating a specific rule. So, is the "agreement" limited to addressing the homeowner's "guilt" or "innocence" of that charge and whether there will be a fine or not (if "guilty")? Or can it be broader in scope? For example, can the "agreement" require the homeowner to pay the board's legal fees (because boards will likely have their attorneys present at all hearings because of this requirement)? Can the "agreement" address issues beyond the scope of the notice that preceded the hearing?

- **Whether the homeowner has the right to have an attorney present at the hearing before the homeowner signs such**

an "agreement." The fact that AB 130 is silent on this issue raises two giant problems. First, since the statute says nothing about allowing homeowners to have an attorney with them at such hearings almost certainly means that the existing law on the subject remains the same—i.e., homeowners do not have the right to have an attorney present at a disciplinary hearing. That omission leads directly into the second problem. If, in fact, it's now mandatory that the board and homeowner must draft a written resolution (i.e., the "agreement"), and if that "agreement" is now judicially enforceable, meaning that it can be enforced by a court according to its terms, then how can a homeowner be prevented from having an attorney present to review the "agreement" and advise the homeowner?[7]

The sad thing is that none of this was necessary. If a member and the board at a pre-AB 130 hearing wanted to formally settle a dispute (instead of moving forward with a warning or a fine), they already had the right to do that, and the Davis-Stirling Act already contained a provision stating that such agreements would be enforceable by a court. In my opinion, therefore, by inserting this language into the middle of the disciplinary process, AB 130 has done nothing but create confusion and the potential for a serious due process problem for homeowners who are not equipped to protect their own rights.

---

7. I recognize that 5855 does not state that the "agreement" has to be drafted and signed at the meeting, but for practical purposes that I won't get into in this book, I see that interpretation as a distinct possibility. And whether I'm wrong or right isn't the point. The point is, that the statute is not clear about it, meaning that some HOAs will interpret it that way, and others won't (in which case, a homeowner will have the chance to have an attorney advise them, and it won't present a due process problem). It's the potential due process issue that concerns me here.

What AB 130 Actually Requires: A Procedural Checklist

After all the ambiguity, one question still matters most: What does AB 130 actually require? Here's the current state of the law, broken down step by step:

- **Advance written notice of the alleged violation.** AB 130 made no changes to the requirement that the board notify the member about the hearing in writing. The notice must still include the date, time, and location of the hearing, a description of the alleged violation, and a statement that the member has the right to attend and be heard. The notice must either be (a) personally delivered, or (b) sent via first-class mail, or, if the member explicitly confirmed in writing, by email or other electronic means.

- **The board must cancel the hearing.** The board must cancel the hearing if the member either cures the violation or submits a financial commitment to cure it before the scheduled hearing.

- **The hearing must be held in executive session.** AB 130 made no changes to the requirement that disciplinary hearings be held in private, outside the presence of other members, and allow the homeowner to appear and be heard. This isn't a public shaming session or a silent rubber stamp. The homeowner has the right to respond to the allegations directly.

- **If the board and the member do not reach agreement at the hearing, the member has the right to request IDR.** If the board and the member do not reach agreement at the hearing, the member has the right to request Internal Dispute Resolution under Civil Code section 5910 (a right that already existed even if it was unstated in the old version of the statute).

- **If the board and the member do reach an agreement.** If the board and the member do reach agreement, the board must draft a written resolution. If both parties sign it, the agreement becomes judicially enforceable.

- **The board must provide written notice of its decision within 14 days of the hearing.** This replaced the old 15-day rule. So now, the notice to the homeowner must go out within 14 days of the hearing. As was the case before, the notice requirement applies to all disciplinary actions, including fines and privilege suspensions.

- **HOAs may no longer add interest or late fees to unpaid fines.** AB 130 prohibits HOAs from charging interest, late fees, or penalties on unpaid fines.

Each of these steps is now a legal prerequisite to enforcement. If the board skips even one, whether through omission, misunderstanding, or deliberate shortcut, the penalty is likely unenforceable.

What's So Special About a Formal ADR Demand Letter?

A lot of our clients ask us to "just send a quick demand letter" to their HOA, and we almost always explain why that's a mistake.

Your HOA or management company can completely ignore a regular demand letter. There's absolutely no legal consequence for blowing it off.

But an ADR demand letter, brought under the auspices of Civil Code §§ 5925 to 5940, can't be ignored so easily. *That* letter triggers formal legal obligations, including strict deadlines for the HOA to respond or participate in mediation. And if they blow off that letter, their decision can come back to bite them.

Assuming that this case involves an award of attorney's fees and costs to the winning party, and it's likely that it will, then if the HOA were to somehow win the lawsuit, Civil Code § 5960 gives the judge the power to substantially reduce the amount of its attorney's fees based solely on your HOA's refusal to participate in ADR when you offered it to them.

And here's another strategic advantage: if the HOA doesn't send back its own ADR demand, then the only issues that can be discussed at mediation are the ones you raised in your demand. That means that you control the narrative.

DISPUTE RESOLUTION
(IDR AND ADR)

D ISPUTES BETWEEN HOMEOWNERS and HOA boards are inevitable. Often, they involve fines or architectural denials. Other times they center on maintenance issues, access to records, or board conduct. But no matter the topic, there's a separate layer of law that governs how those disputes must be handled.

The Davis-Stirling Act lays out two separate processes to address homeowner/association disputes: Internal Dispute Resolution and Alternative Dispute Resolution. Both can dramatically affect the outcome of a conflict, especially if a homeowner misunderstands when these procedures apply, what rights they have, or how the board might exploit the process to gain the upper hand.

This chapter breaks down everything you need to know about IDR and ADR in the HOA context, from which one is voluntary, to when the law requires the parties to participate, to what happens if a party refuses. It explains how HOAs routinely misstate the law, delay enforcement, or ambush homeowners into lopsided settlement talks under the false banner of "required dispute resolution." Most important, it gives you the strategic insight to recognize the traps and take control of the process before your rights are waived.

What Is IDR and When Does It Apply?

IDR is an informal "meet and confer" process available to members and HOAs to try to work out disputes without the need for escalation. Under Civil Code section 5905, an association may use a simple procedure that amounts to a prompt sit-down with one or more directors to discuss the dispute. There is no judge, no mediator, and no neutral third party unless both sides agree to bring one in, which is uncommon. The HOA cannot charge any fees or costs for IDR. Each side may bring an attorney at its own expense, but most IDRs take place without counsel present. If one side does bring an attorney, the other is entitled to do the same.

IDR is also limited by its informality. It is not designed to resolve complex or heavily contested disputes. Because there is no neutral decision-maker, no evidence rules, and no binding result, IDR works best for minor disagreements or as a way to document that the board is unwilling to compromise. If the issue involves significant money, legal complexity, or entrenched hostility, IDR alone is unlikely to be effective.

Under Civil Code section 5915, an HOA must participate in IDR if a homeowner requests it. The reverse is not true. But that hasn't stopped some HOAs from claiming otherwise, either by misreading the statute or pointing to governing documents that require *both* parties to engage in IDR. To the extent that your HOA's governing documents require you to engage in IDR, those provisions are unenforceable because they directly conflict with the Davis-Stirling Act.

As indicated above, most HOAs rely on section 5905's minimal framework rather than adopting any plan that uses a paid neutral. That keeps IDRs informal, quick, and entirely board-controlled, which is why homeowners should be selective about when to use it and when to not bother wasting their time.

In many situations, there are strategic reasons a homeowner might request IDR. In some cases, it can reveal a reasonable board willing to resolve a problem without the need for escalation. In others, it can be used to document the board's refusal to engage in good faith, which may help later in court. But IDR is not the right move in every case, especially when the board is hostile, the issue is legally complex, or the association has already retained litigation counsel.

In short, when it comes to IDR, homeowners control the decision, not HOAs. HOAs cannot force you to request IDR. They cannot penalize you for declining it. And they cannot falsely claim that you've waived your rights just because you chose to proceed directly to court or with more formal ADR.

What is ADR and When Does It Apply?

IDR may be optional for homeowners, but ADR is an entirely different matter. In many HOA disputes, ADR is either legally required before you can file a lawsuit or strategically recommended because of its potential to resolve a case quickly and cost-effectively. Before we dive into the rules and timelines, let's be clear about what ADR actually is, and what it isn't.

Understanding ADR in the HOA Context

Before going further, and because terminology matters, it's important to be precise about what "ADR" means in the context of HOA disputes. Technically, ADR includes both mediation and arbitration. And while a lot of laypeople, and even some sloppy attorneys, use "arbitration" and "mediation" interchangeably, they are fundamentally different processes with entirely different outcomes.

Mediation is just a fancy word for settlement discussions. It is not binding. There are no witnesses testifying, no rules of evidence to follow, no depositions being conducted, and no judges or juries making any findings/decisions. It is simply formal settlement discussions being conducted in front of a neutral person, typically a retired judge or experienced attorney. Each side participating in mediation pays half of the mediator's fees, and if they have their own attorneys, they each pay for their own attorneys as well.

While mediation is, as I said above, a fancy word for settlement discussions, arbitration is essentially a private trial process agreed to by parties to a contract. It is synonymous with suing someone in court. In arbitration, the roles of judge and jury are taken by an arbitrator, who hears the case and issues a decision. Although some contracts requiring arbitration state that the arbitration is non-binding—in which case if a party isn't happy with the arbitrator's decision, that party can reject it and the case moves to the regular court system—most arbitrations are binding. That means the arbitrator's decision is final, with virtually no right to appeal. That decision can then be filed with the superior court, at which point it becomes a judgment. That judgment is the same judgment that one would get after going to trial in court.

In the context of most HOA disputes, the term "ADR" typically refers to mediation, and for the purpose of this book, it will as well.

When ADR is Required and When it Isn't (and Why We Almost Always Recommend it Anyway)

Under Civil Code section 5930, mediation is required before a homeowner or HOA can file a lawsuit (or demand for arbitration) in certain enforcement actions. The requirement applies if the lawsuit is both: (a) intended to enforce the governing documents; and (b) seeks only declaratory, injunctive, or writ relief, or seeks those remedies along with money damages of $12,500 or less.

In all other instances, the Davis-Stirling Act does *not* require mediation or any other form of ADR.

But when mediation is required and a party refuses to participate, there can be real consequences. Civil Code section 5960 authorizes the court to consider that refusal when deciding how much to award in attorney's fees and costs (which Civil Code section 5975(c) requires the court to award to the prevailing party in an enforcement action). A refusal to mediate when required can result in the judge significantly, though not completely, reducing the prevailing party's right to recover attorney's fees if that party failed to participate in ADR when it was required under the Davis-Stirling Act.

The ADR statute also includes a procedural compliance requirement. Civil Code section 5950 requires the party filing suit to include, with the initial pleading, a certificate stating that ADR has been completed or that the other side refused to participate. If that certificate is missing, the defendant can demur and ask the court to dismiss the case for non-compliance. In practical terms, this means that even if you are the plaintiff and you fail to offer ADR, or you refuse to participate when the HOA offered it, your case could be derailed before the court ever reaches the merits. Although the derailment might only be temporary, because you could complete ADR and then refile, you will still have wasted time and money unnecessarily.

Even when mediation isn't legally required, however, we almost always recommend it. The reasons are straightforward. First, mediation is orders of magnitude less expensive than litigation. Second, using the legal processes that I developed when I pioneered this niche area of the law, my firm's settlement rate at the pre-litigation stage increased to well over 50%. That fact, coupled with a strategic benefit that most homeowners don't think about, makes ADR an excellent investment in terms of money and time. And what is that strategic benefit?

Simple. We can often negotiate remedies that a court could never order, even if you were to win at trial. For example, we have successfully negotiated the removal of abusive or disruptive directors, sometimes permanently and sometimes for a set period of time, as part of resolving a dispute via a settlement agreement negotiated during the pre-litigation ADR process. This is not a remedy a judge or jury could grant in a typical enforcement lawsuit unless there was an explicit statutory basis for that person's inability to serve. Courts generally don't interfere with an HOA's "democratic process." But in settlement, the parties can agree to anything that's lawful and mutually acceptable. That kind of flexibility, combined with the cost savings and higher likelihood of early resolution, makes ADR a good investment in most situations. Plus, if the case doesn't settle, and instead proceeds to trial, under the Davis-Stirling Act, the prevailing party will be entitled to their pre-litigation attorneys' fees, so they'll be able to recoup the money spent during the ADR process.

Case Study

One of our clients asked us to challenge the HOA after it denied his request for an exterior improvement. The board insisted it had complete discretion and refused to change its decision. Most homeowners treat ADR as a pointless step before litigation. We use it as a weapon.

We built the record before we served our ADR demand. We documented other owners who received approval for similar improvements while the board singled out our client. We pulled association records and uncovered financial inconsistencies. That gave us two pressure points to use against the HOA: selective enforcement and financial mismanagement.

We framed those risks in the ADR demand we prepared for our client. We told the board it could grant approval now or face a selective enforcement lawsuit that would include financial claims and attorney's fees. The board understood that fighting us meant turning one variance dispute into a community-wide scandal.

At mediation, the board caved. Our client got his approval, and the dispute ended. ADR gave us the setting to flip the risk back onto the HOA and force the result our client wanted. We even negotiated reimbursement of 75% of our client's attorney's fees even though that isn't a requirement at the ADR stage.

Pre-Litigation ADR Timelines Under the Davis-Stirling Act

Let's assume that you've decided to engage in pre-litigation ADR. The Davis-Stirling Act sets strict timelines for how the process must start and how long it can last.

- **Step 1: Serving a Written Request for ADR.** Under Civil Code section 5935, the party initiating ADR must serve the other side with a "Request for Resolution." The ADR demand may be sent in a variety of ways provided that the sender is reasonably sure that the receiving party will get the demand. Under Civil Code section 5935, the ADR demand must:

  — Briefly describe the dispute.

  — State that the requesting party is seeking to resolve the dispute through ADR (and in our ADR demands, we specify that we're explicitly demanding mediation).

  — Tell the recipient that they have 30 days to respond.[1]

- **Step 2: The 30-Day Response Deadline.** Once the ADR demand goes out, the recipient has 30 days to accept or reject it in writing. If they fail to respond within that time, the law treats the silence as a rejection (Civ. Code, § 5935(c)).

- **Step 3: Completing ADR Within 90 Days.** If the other party accepts the ADR demand, then Civil Code section 5940 requires that the ADR be completed within 90 days of acceptance, unless the parties agree in writing to extend the deadline. If the request is rejected, or if the ADR is not completed within the 90-day period (and no written extension is signed), either party is free

---

1. If the HOA is the party demanding ADR with a member, the HOA must also provide a copy of Civil Code section 5935 to the member.

to proceed with litigation. This is designed to reduce the opportunities for the opposing side to play games and waste time.

ADR under the Davis-Stirling Act is confidential (Evid. Code, §§ 1115–1128). Nothing said or done in mediation can be used later in court, and the mediator cannot be subpoenaed to testify.

Civil Code section 5940(c) requires the costs of ADR to be shared equally, unless the parties agree otherwise, and each side is responsible for its own attorney's fees for the mediation itself unless a different arrangement is negotiated as part of a settlement.

Why You Need to Have a Qualified Attorney Represent You in ADR

Unlike a typical demand letter that any HOA board can simply ignore, a formal ADR demand letter brought under the auspices of Civil Code sections 5925 to 5940, can't be ignored so easily. It triggers formal legal obligations, including strict deadlines for the HOA to respond or participate in mediation. If your HOA ignores a plain demand letter, there is no consequence. But if your HOA ignores a formal ADR demand letter, that refusal can come back to bite them.

Let's assume for a moment that pre-litigation mediation does not result in a settlement, and instead the case progresses to litigation. And let's assume that somehow, your HOA wins at trial. Assuming that your case involves an award of attorney's fees to the prevailing party (as most will under the Davis-Stirling Act), your HOA's refusal to participate in ADR when you gave them the chance to could result in the judge significantly reducing the amount of their attorney's fees award based on their refusal to participate (Civ. Code, § 5960).

Which leads us to another point. While laypeople are perfectly equipped to participate effectively in IDR (if they feel it will yield positive results), the same is not true for formal ADR demands. If your dispute has escalated to the point where a formal ADR demand is necessary or appropriate, then you would be wise to hire an attorney with expertise in HOA law to represent you.

Unlike IDR, mediation often addresses disputes involving substantial sums of money and complex legal issues, including the potential for fee-shifting under the Davis-Stirling Act. Going into mediation without a lawyer can be a serious disadvantage, potentially causing you to miss opportunities for leverage, unintentionally forfeit crucial rights, or settle for terms that are much less favorable than the law provides.

Making ADR Work for You: Strategy, Risks, and Common Mistakes

ADR can be one of the most powerful tools a homeowner has for resolving an HOA dispute, but only if it's approached strategically. In my firm's experience, pre-litigation mediation is successful more often than not. This means that our firm is typically able to resolve the dispute without ever having to file a lawsuit. Consequently, unless there's an excellent reason to skip that step, we almost always recommend that our clients try ADR before resorting to a lawsuit.

That said, homeowners must also be aware that some boards misuse ADR. They may attend mediation only to posture, delay, or drive up costs, hoping the homeowner will give up. This is yet another reason why approaching ADR with counsel and a clear plan is so important.

But there are other reasons to try ADR before suing. As I explained previously, mediation gives you opportunities that you won't get in court. You can negotiate creative solutions, set timelines for compliance, address underlying issues that might not be worth litigating (but which might still be helpful in fully resolving your dispute), or even negotiate concessions that would otherwise be legally unavailable to you if you filed a lawsuit and won at trial.

ADR isn't, however, always the right choice. In those cases where ADR is not required under the Davis-Stirling Act, it might not be worth pursuing notwithstanding its statistical benefits. For example, assuming that it's not a required hoop to jump through, we might recommend skipping pre-litigation ADR (and moving directly to litigation) if:

- **You're dealing with a particularly hostile board.** In some cases, the personalities involved have rendered the relationships so toxic, and the egos of the individuals involved are so intertwined with the dispute, that there is little chance of a peaceful resolution during pre-litigation.

- **The HOA's attorney has proved unable to exercise "client control."** In an ideal world, the attorneys hired by HOAs to advise and represent them are not only experts in the Davis-Stirling Act, but also capable of exercising what attorneys call "client control." Client control refers to an attorney's ability to rein in a client who is acting on emotion rather than common sense, who is ignoring the realities of what the law allows (versus what the client wants), or who is insisting on pursuing an unethical course of conduct. In practice, many HOA-side attorneys fail at exerting client control, and they allow their clients to act in a manner that is contrary to the law and to the best interests of the HOA as a whole. In such cases, ADR is often not worth it, so if it's not required by the Davis-Stirling Act, it might be better to skip it and move directly to litigation.

Used intelligently, ADR can be a cost-effective, low-risk way to resolve even the most entrenched HOA disputes.

CAN NON-OWNERS SERVE ON MY HOA'S BOARD?

No. Under California law, only members of the association can serve on the HOA board.

And the definition of "member" is specific when it comes to the Davis-Stirling Act. A "member" is someone who has a validly *recorded* ownership interest in the property. An unrecorded deed granting any percentage of ownership to someone is not sufficient to establish "membership" for Davis-Stirling Act purposes.

That's not just a best practice, it's the law. Civil Code § 5105(b) requires HOAs to disqualify any board candidate who isn't a member at the time of nomination.

So renters, property managers, family members, holders of unrecorded deeds (sometimes called "pocket deeds"), or anyone else who doesn't hold recorded title cannot serve, even if they've lived in the community for years or used to serve on the board before that particular law changed.

If your HOA has non-owners on the board, they're violating state law, and any actions they take could be challenged as invalid.

So yes, board service is limited to owners. And if that's not what's happening in your HOA, it's a serious problem.

BOARD ELECTIONS
AND MEMBER VOTING

D IRECTOR ELECTIONS ARE the most powerful tool homeowners have to shape the future of their HOA. The people who sit on your HOA's board of directors decide how your money is spent, what the rules should be and how they should be enforced, and whether your rights as a homeowner are respected or ignored. If the wrong people hold those seats, your HOA can become an unaccountable machine that runs on secrecy, favoritism, or outright abuse.

In this chapter, "elections" means the process of electing your HOA's board of directors. We are not talking here about member votes to amend the CC&Rs, change the use of common areas, or approve special assessments. Those types of votes have their own separate rules under California law, and are not covered in this chapter.

The focus here is on the statutory framework for board elections under Civil Code sections 5100 through 5145. You'll learn the notice and nomination requirements, how ballots must be handled, and the safeguards the law puts in place to ensure fair elections. You'll also see how boards and their allies try to manipulate these rules and what you can do to stop them.

For homeowners, understanding these rules is more than a matter of curiosity. It's a matter of control. A fair election process is the only way to ensure that the board reflects the will of the membership, not just a small group determined to stay in power.

Why HOA Elections Matter

Director elections determine who will run the association for the next term. Your board makes decisions about *everything* related to the management of your HOA, from maintenance and spending, to enforcement and policy. They control the association's budget, decide whether to increase dues or levy special assessments, and direct the association's attorney in disputes with homeowners. In other words, they manage both the financial and legal health of the HOA.

Because the board wields so much authority, the composition of that board matters. A lot.

A board committed to transparency, fairness, and compliance with the law can protect property values and improve community life. A bad HOA board driven by self-interest or petty grievances can cause years of conflict, financial waste, and legal trouble. Stated far more simply, a good HOA will help your pocketbook. An HOA from Hell will hurt your pocketbook.

Low turnout, apathy, or manipulation of the process can cement power in the hands of a small group. In many cases, those who benefit from staying in control will work hard to discourage competition, control the flow of information, and make the process as confusing as possible. Knowing your rights and the rules for how elections must be conducted is the first step in preventing this.

Elections are also one of the few areas in which the membership directly influences the governance of their association. Once directors are elected, they may be difficult to remove before their terms expire, even if they later act in ways the membership doesn't support. That's why fair elections, and homeowner participation in them, are essential to keeping the association accountable.

Candidate Qualifications and Disqualifications

California law is crystal clear on the subject of who may run for and serve on an HOA's board. Only members of the association are eligible to do either of those things. "Member" means you hold a *recorded* ownership interest in a separate interest within the development. If your name is not on a recorded deed, the HOA may not treat you as a member, and thus for purposes of the Davis-Stirling Act, you can't vote or serve on the board. This comes up often in the case of family trusts, intra-family transfers, divorce settlements, and "pocket deed" situations where the parties never bothered recording the transfer/ownership documents.

From there, Civil Code section 5105 allows an HOA to impose certain disqualifications, but only if they are written into the HOA's election rules well before the election begins. These include:

- **Assessment delinquencies**. A member can be disqualified for not paying regular or special assessments, but only if (a) the same rule applies to sitting directors, and (b) the delinquent member isn't paying under an approved payment plan.

- **Minimum ownership period**. Requiring that a candidate has owned their unit or lot for at least one year.

- **One owner per unit or lot**. If multiple people own the same unit or lot, only one of them can serve on the board at a time.

- **Certain criminal convictions**. Disqualification for a criminal conviction is allowed only if the conviction would prevent the HOA from purchasing the fidelity bond required by Civil Code section 5806.

Any other disqualification, no matter how reasonable it sounds, is unenforceable. HOAs cannot, therefore, prevent someone from running for or serving on the board because they:

- Haven't paid their fines.

- Are in litigation with the HOA.

- Have a felony conviction that doesn't affect the fidelity bond.

- Are too young to live in the community (such as a 20-year-old who inherits title to a home in a 55-and-older HOA).

Anyone disqualified from running or serving for an improper reason has the ability to challenge the disqualification. Under Civil Code section 5105, the HOA must give written notice of disqualification and offer IDR at least 40 days before ballots are mailed.

Balloting and Voting Procedures

Once the candidate list is finalized, the HOA must run the election by secret ballot under the supervision of one or three independent inspectors of election. I discuss the role of those independent inspectors in the next section of this chapter.

Equal Access to Media and Facilities

During that time frame, the candidates who have announced themselves may campaign to their fellow HOA members. The Davis-Stirling Act protects campaign speech and member organizing (Civ. Code, § 5105). Under member speech protections, homeowners have the right to canvass, distribute literature, use social media, and peacefully assemble in common areas for election-related meetings, subject to reasonable time, place, and manner rules. Boards may not retaliate against members for engaging in protected election activity, and they cannot impose any restrictions that favor incumbents..

Likewise, if the association uses its newsletters, website, or other association media for campaign purposes, Civil Code section 5105 requires that all candidates and advocates be given equal access on the same terms. And if the board makes common area facilities available for private campaign purposes, it must extend the same right to challengers.

Envelopes and Ballots

Each homeowner receives a ballot along with two envelopes:

- The inner envelope will contain the completed ballot.

- The outer envelope will contain the voter's name, address, and signature.

The inner envelope containing the ballot will be sealed inside the outer one. It contains the ballot only. There is not supposed to be any information on either the ballot or the inner envelope that could identify the member who casts the ballot. The outer envelope, which includes the name, address, and signature of the voting member, allows the inspector to confirm that the person voting is eligible. Once verified, the inspector must store the unopened inner envelopes containing the ballots until the election meeting.

Completed ballots must be mailed directly to the inspector of election or to a location the inspector designates. If the board directs homeowners to send ballots to the HOA office or to a board member, that violates Civil Code section 5115. The inspector is required to keep the ballots secure from the time they are received until the vote count is complete. The inspector must open and count them in public view at a properly noticed meeting.

Members have the right to observe the tabulation in real time. During the count, the independent inspector is responsible for verifying eligibility, resolving challenges, and ensuring secrecy is maintained. If issues arise during the count, such as questions about a signature on the outer envelope or eligibility to vote, *the inspector, not the board*, must resolve them. And whatever rules are applied must be applied uniformly to all ballots.

Quorums

In California HOA board elections, the governing documents typically specify the quorum requirement, which is the minimum number of members who must cast ballots for the election to be valid. Quorum is usually defined as a percentage of the total voting power of the association, usually a majority (i.e., 51%), though the exact percentage can vary depending on the Bylaws. Once a quorum is reached, the winner of a board seat is the candidate who receives the most votes out of that quorum, not a majority of all members. If quorum is not achieved, the ballots cannot be counted and the election is invalid, meaning that the current directors continue serving until a valid election is held or a reduced quorum provision (if one exists in the Bylaws) allows the election to proceed.

Custody of the Ballots & One-Year Statute of Limitations

After the election, the inspector must keep the ballots for at least one year. This allows homeowners to review them if there's a dispute about the results. Homeowners are entitled to inspect the ballots, signed outer envelopes, and tally sheets during that one-year period, subject to the protections that preserve ballot secrecy (Civ. Code, § 5125). This right ensures transparency after the fact. By comparing the tally sheets, signatures, and ballot counts, members can independently confirm the integrity of the election or gather evidence to support a challenge under Civil Code section 5145. The one-year retention period aligns with Civil Code section 5145, which gives homeowners only one year to challenge the results of an election. After that period expires, both the right to inspect and the right to contest the outcome expire forever.

Civil Code section 5145 also authorizes statutory penalties of up to $500 per violation, along with attorney's fees and costs, giving homeowners real leverage in enforcing election fairness. But what makes this particular statute especially unusual is that the Legislature expressly extended fee recovery even to prevailing parties in *small claims court* (after, for example, consulting with an attorney to help them prepare for the small claims trial)—something that no other provision of the Davis-Stirling Act does.

Electronic Voting (Effective January 1, 2025)

As of January 1, 2025, HOAs in California may, though are not required to, conduct elections using electronic secret ballots. AB 2159 affected key provisions of the Davis-Stirling Act dealing with elections and balloting.

Electronic voting follows the same principles as paper ballots, but the law now requires extra protections to make sure technology doesn't compromise secrecy or fairness. For example, Civil Code section 5110(c) now includes additional duties for the inspectors of election, who must now ensure that:

- Homeowners can authenticate their identity to the system securely.

- Ballots are submitted in a way that protects their secrecy and integrity.

- At least 30 days before the voting deadline, homeowners are able to test their devices to confirm they work with the system.

- The system:

  — Authenticates voter identity.

  — Verifies each ballot's validity and protects against tampering.

  — Sends a receipt to each voter confirming submission.

  — Separates identifiable information from ballots so votes cannot be traced back to specific homeowners.

  — Preserves electronic ballots so they remain accessible for audits, recounts, or reviews.

These requirements mirror the protections already in place for paper ballots, but adapted to the digital age. Boards that cut corners on these safeguards put the entire election at risk of being invalidated.

Election Oversight and Inspectors

Every HOA election must be overseen by either one or three independent inspectors of election. Inspectors of election are the referees of the HOA election process, so their role is not symbolic. They are the ones who ensure the legitimacy of the election outcome by making sure that only eligible voters' ballots are counted, that ballots are handled properly, and that everyone's vote remains confidential.

The law requires the board to choose either one or three inspectors, and the inspector must be appointed before ballots are mailed. This timing matters because the ballot instructions must tell members exactly where to return their completed ballots, and that address must belong to the inspector or a location chosen by the inspector. The ballot cannot be sent to either the board or the management company.

The Davis-Stirling Act allows a range of people to serve as inspectors of election, so long as they are independent. Inspectors may be fellow HOA members who are not on the ballot, certified public accountants, attorneys, or professional election service vendors. That flexibility stops where conflicts of interest begin. Inspectors cannot be current board members, candidates in the election, their relatives, the association's management company, or anyone with a financial stake in the outcome.

Once appointed, inspectors control the entire election process. Their duties include:

- Verifying the accuracy of the voter list.

- Receiving and safeguarding ballots until the official count.

- Opening ballots in public view at a properly noticed meeting.

- Counting and certifying the results.

- Retaining the ballots for at least one year after the election.

It should go without saying that the more familiar an inspector is with his or her election-related obligations under the Davis-Stirling Act, the better he or she can do his or her job. For that reason, even though any independent adult can serve as an inspector, a lot of HOAs turn to "professional" inspectors to manage their elections.

When an HOA board appoints inspectors in a timely fashion and lets them carry out their duties, the election process works as intended. But if the board delays appointments, reroutes ballots back through itself, or selects inspectors with obvious conflicts, it compromises election legitimacy. In those cases, Civil Code section 5110 empowers homeowners to challenge the election results.

Common Election Abuses and How to Spot Them

Knowing the rules is one thing. But even with clear legal requirements in place, many HOA boards still find ways to manipulate the election process. Recognizing when your board is breaking those rules is critical to holding it accountable. Bad HOAs cut corners and bend procedures in ways that tilt elections toward incumbents or favored candidates.

Some of these tactics are deliberate, others careless, but either way they put the integrity of the election at risk.

The most common abuses to look out for include:

- **Burying nomination forms.** Boards may circulate nomination paperwork late or inconsistently so that only incumbents meet the deadline.

- **Inventing disqualification rules.** Directors may try to keep challengers off the ballot by applying restrictions that California law does not allow.

- **Violating ballot secrecy**. Bad HOA boards sometimes try meddling with the required ballot confidentiality by adding names, unit numbers, or voting codes on ballots or inner envelopes to make it possible to connect a homeowner to a vote.

- **Choosing conflicted inspectors**. Boards sometimes appoint friends, relatives, or even their management company as inspectors, even though inspectors must be independent.

- **Blocking access to member lists**. Challengers can't campaign effectively if the board refuses to provide the membership list when requested—something that your HOA is required to provide if you request it.

- **Manipulating the vote count**. Boards may fail to give proper notice of the tabulation meeting, change the location at the last minute, or arrange for a non-independent inspector to count ballots outside of the public view.

- **Rushing or delaying the process**. California law requires elections to follow a strict schedule of notices and deadlines. When boards start the process too late, amend rules too close to the election, or skip required steps, they jeopardize the entire election. Suffice it to say that the election preparation period should start at least 120 days before the election (or more in the case of electronic voting) to ensure that timelines are properly followed.

- **Misusing association funds for campaigns**. Civil Code section 5135 prohibits directors from using HOA money, staff, or resources to support their personal campaigns. Bad HOA directors often ignore that prohibition.

- **Blocking access to HOA facilities**. Bad HOAs sometimes allow their incumbent directors to utilize HOA facilities (like clubhouses) for their own campaign events while violating the

Davis-Stirling Act by denying challengers equal access to the same HOA-owned common areas.

These tactics undermine the fairness of the election process. That's why it's so important for HOA members like you to watch closely, document what happens, and keep copies of notices, envelopes, and ballots. By building a solid paper trail, you strengthen your position if you ever need to challenge the results of the election.

Case Study

A group of homeowners came to us after noticing a series of very suspicious incidents at a recent board election. Apparently, several ballots had been thrown out for "technical errors," including envelopes the inspector claimed were missing signatures even though signatures were clearly visible. The board moved quickly to certify the results, which kept the incumbents in power.

We demanded access to the ballots and tally sheets under Civil Code section 5125. When we inspected them, the problem became obvious. The board's inspector had rejected valid ballots cast by members who opposed the sitting directors. Those votes would have changed the outcome.

We put the board on notice: certify the tainted results or we would sue under Civil Code section 5145, seeking to invalidate the election, impose statutory penalties, and recover attorney's fees. Faced with that risk, the board agreed to rerun the election with a new, independent inspector.

The second election flipped control. Reform candidates won, and the new board immediately stopped a controversial spending project that was going to beautify the building where two of the directors lived. For those homeowners, catching election misconduct wasn't about principle. It was about protecting their money and changing the direction of the community.

Recalling a Bad HOA Board

In California, few tools are as decisive, and as underused, as the HOA recall. When a homeowners association board stops following the law, ignores the membership, or simply refuses to act in the community's best interest, the Davis-Stirling Act gives homeowners a direct and powerful remedy: *remove them from office*.

Under the Davis–Stirling Act and the California Corporations Code, the recall process is designed to be accessible. In most HOAs, it takes signatures from only 5% of the membership to trigger a mandatory special election. That low threshold exists to give homeowners a practical way to hold their board accountable without waiting for the next regular election cycle.

But initiating a recall is not as simple as circulating a petition and counting signatures. The process has strict statutory requirements for how the petition is written, how signatures are gathered and verified, and how the election itself is conducted. A single procedural misstep can give the board a pretext to reject the petition or derail the election altogether.

This part of the chapter explains exactly how HOA recall petitions work in California, from the legal thresholds, to the strategic decisions that can determine whether your recall effort succeeds. It also addresses the most common tactics boards use to resist removal, and how to protect your rights at every stage of the process. By understanding the law and planning your approach, you can use the recall as it was intended: to restore accountability and integrity to your HOA's leadership.

Why Recalling the Entire Board is Recommended

When initiating a recall, California homeowners have the option to target one or more individual directors or to recall the entire board. While it might seem logical to focus only on the directors causing the most problems, in most situations it is strategically better to recall all directors at once.

The primary reason is cumulative voting, which is the default method of voting in the majority of California HOAs. If your HOA does not have cumulative voting, then this recommendation doesn't apply. But if your HOA is like most of the ones in California, then this is a big deal. Under cumulative voting, members are allowed to "stack" all of their votes on a single candidate.

This makes a difference because under Corporations Code section 7222(b)(1), in a recall where cumulative voting is in effect, no director may be removed if the votes cast against removal would be enough to elect the director if voted cumulatively at an election where all the members entitled to vote were voted. This is an extremely high bar to meet.

When the entire board is up for recall, however, the cumulative voting rules do not come into play. Instead, the threshold vote will depend on the size of your HOA.

- **Associations with less than 50 members.** In associations with fewer than 50 members, the recall will be approved if a majority of the members entitled to vote decide to remove the board (i.e., they approve the recall). For example, if your association has 30 members, then you would need at least 16 members to vote in favor of the recall. This means that if only a mere quorum showed up to vote (i.e., if only 16 members voted), just one "no" vote would be enough to prevent the recall because at least 16 members have to vote in favor of the recall for it to pass.

- **Associations with more than 50 members**. If the HOA has more than 50 members, then the recall will be successful if a majority of a quorum voted to remove the board. For example, if your association has 60 members, then 31 would constitute quorum. If only 31 people showed up to vote in the recall, you could remove the board with the vote of just 16—the same number as the example above in the smaller association because 16 represents a majority of the quorum (which was 31).

In most cases, therefore, removing the entire board as opposed to select members is far easier and more often successful. Even if your real target is just one or two board members, you should seek to remove the entire board and then campaign in favor of reelecting the remaining good ones, plus the one or two you nominate to replace the bad directors.[1]

Understanding the Legal Framework for Recalls

In California, the right to recall HOA board members is not vague or symbolic. It is a statutory right rooted in the Davis–Stirling Act and the California Corporations Code. Both sets of statutes apply, and the applicable sections of both must be understood to execute a valid recall.

- **The Davis-Stirling Act and HOA Recall Elections**. Under Civil Code section 5100(a)(1), any HOA election to remove directors must be conducted by secret ballot and comply with

---

1. This particular issue is so badly addressed in both the Corporations Code and in the Davis-Stirling Act, that there is actually a difference of opinion amongst experts and courts as to how to interpret or reconcile the language. This, therefore, serves as another reason why you want to avoid cumulative voting by seeking the recall of the entire board instead of one or more (but not all) of the directors.

the same procedural safeguards that apply to regular board elections. This includes:

— Double-envelope system to ensure ballot security.

— Independent inspector(s) of election to oversee the process.

— Notices and nomination periods consistent with statutory timelines.

There's a lot of confusion, however, regarding the election timeline associated with recall petitions because it's not the same as with regular elections. While the Davis–Stirling Act controls the how of the voting process, the when is driven by the California Corporations Code. If cumulative voting applies, the board must give notice of the recall meeting within 20 days of receiving a valid petition. The meeting itself must occur between 35 and 150 days after receipt. If cumulative voting does not apply, the meeting must occur between 120 and 150 days, which is the practical window associations use to comply with the Corporations Code's 35-150 day requirement while also meeting the Davis-Stirling Act's secret-ballot notice and mailing timelines. In either case, Civil Code section 5115 still applies, requiring that ballots be mailed or delivered to all members at least 30 days before the voting deadline.[2]

So, the Davis–Stirling Act's normal pre-election planning windows do not apply here. Rather, the recall must be scheduled

2. There are special rules for HOAs that have adopted electronic voting. The deadline is a bit different if your HOA has adopted electronic voting under the new law that went into effect in California on January 1, 2025. In HOAs that have adopted electronic voting, the meeting date is set 150 days after receipt of the recall petition. Likewise, in HOAs with electronic voting, ballots must be sent at least 15 days before the voting deadline rather than the 30 days required for paper ballots. But since most HOAs have not yet adopted electronic voting, this book is focused on the rules applicable to HOAs still relying on paper ballots.

within that timeframe contained in the Corporations Code while still meeting the Davis–Stirling Act's minimum 30-day ballot period.

Failure to follow those steps can invalidate the recall election entirely, and in some cases expose the HOA to statutory penalties and attorney's fees.

- **The Corporations Code and HOA Recall Elections**. The Corporations Code governs the initiation of the recall process. Sections 7510 and 7511 set the procedural requirements for calling a special membership meeting to vote on board removal. Key requirements include:

  — Threshold signatures. For most HOAs, signatures from 5% of the total membership are required to trigger a recall. For stock cooperatives, the threshold is 10%.

  — Delivery. The petition must be delivered to the board, a director, or the association's managing agent, either in person or by certified mail.

  — Timeline. The board must comply with the 20-day notice requirement and set the meeting date in accordance with the applicable 35–150 or 120–150 day range described above.

  — Verification. The association may verify that each signature belongs to an owner of record and that only one signature per unit is counted.

Both statutes matter. Boards, and even some attorneys, often make the mistake of focusing only on Davis–Stirling's election rules. But because the Corporations Code controls how recalls begin, ignoring it can derail the process and give the board an excuse to reject your effort.

How Recall Petitions Work

A recall petition is the legal document that forces the board to schedule a recall election. It is not an informal letter of complaint. The petition must be drafted and executed in compliance with both the Corporations Code and the Davis–Stirling Act, or the board can refuse to act on it.

For most HOAs, the number of signatures required is 5% of the total voting power of the association. This is calculated based on the total number of members entitled to vote, not on the number of households that participate in meetings or recent elections. If calculating 5% produces a fraction, the number is rounded up. If your HOA is a stock cooperative, the threshold is 10%. Stock cooperatives are far less common in California than on the East Coast, but the higher requirement is mandatory if your governing documents classify the development as such.

Only owners of record may sign a recall petition. Co-owners on the same title count as one signature toward the threshold, no matter how many sign. Tenants, non-owner spouses, and other residents who are not on title are not eligible to sign. If one person owns multiple units, they may sign once for each unit owned, and each signature counts separately.

A recurring issue in recall disputes involves "pocket deeds," where a current titleholder has signed over ownership to another person but the deed has not yet been recorded with the county. In most circumstances, a transfer of real property between the grantor and grantee is legally valid even without recordation. For purposes of the Davis–Stirling Act, however, an unrecorded deed is not effective to establish membership rights. This means that the grantee on an unrecorded pocket deed is not recognized as an "owner of record" and cannot sign a recall petition. If a board challenges such a signature, it will be disqualified when the membership roster is compared against recorded title. When collecting signatures, it is critical to confirm that each signer's ownership is reflected in the county recorder's records, especially where a transfer has recently occurred or is in progress, because otherwise you risk falling short of the 5% requirement if those signatures are disqualified.

A valid recall petition must clearly identify the director or directors to be recalled, or state that the entire board is subject to recall. It must demand a special election to vote on removal of those directors and include the printed names, property addresses, and original signatures of the signing members. The Corporations Code requires only a clear statement of purpose and the required member information. Any extra language creates opportunities for the board to argue the petition is ambiguous or defective, so avoid narratives or personal attacks.

Every signature must be original. Photocopies, scanned images, typed names, and e-signatures do not meet the requirement. Best practice is to use blue ink to distinguish original signatures from black-and-white copies. Petition pages may be photocopied for circulation, but the final submission must contain the original signed pages.

The petition must be delivered either in person or by certified mail to the board, a director, or the HOA's managing agent. Certified mail provides a paper trail. Personal delivery should be documented with a written acknowledgment signed and dated by the recipient. I also recommend sending the petition via email as well.

How Recall Elections Work

Once the board receives a valid recall petition and meets the 20-day notice requirement under the Corporations Code, the process shifts to preparing for and conducting the election itself. At this stage, the election must still comply with all of the director election-related procedures required under the Davis–Stirling Act.

The recall election ballot must present two separate questions to the membership:

1. Whether to remove the director(s) named in the petition, or in the case of a full-board recall, whether to remove the entire board.

2. If the recall passes, who should be elected to fill the vacant seats.

Both questions are essential. If the ballot asks only about removal and does not address replacements, and the recall succeeds, the board may have the authority under the Bylaws to appoint new directors itself—potentially reinstating the same individuals or their allies. To prevent that, the replacement election should occur in the same meeting and on the same ballot.

Ballots must follow the double-envelope system required by Civil Code section 5115, and voting must be by secret ballot. An independent inspector of elections must oversee the count. The inspector is also responsible for maintaining the ballots, verifying eligible voters, verifying the quorum, conducting the count, and announcing the results within 15 days of the election.

Keep in mind that once you cast your vote, you cannot revoke or change your vote. Organizers should remind supporters to follow the instructions carefully because errors as simple as forgetting to sign the envelope can cause a ballot to be thrown out, and in a recall, every vote counts.

If the recall passes and enough valid votes are cast for replacements, the newly elected directors are considered elected once the results are certified. Under Corporations Code section 7220(b), however, the prior directors continue to serve until their successors have been "elected and qualified." The timing of qualification, and therefore when the new directors actually take office, depends on the governing documents.

If the recall passes but replacement votes are insufficient to fill all seats, the board may be able to appoint directors to the remaining vacancies, depending on the Bylaws (yet another reason to ensure members complete both parts of the ballot).

Common Ways that Bad HOA Boards Try to Interfere with Recalls

Bad HOA boards will often exploit any weakness in the process to frustrate members' recall efforts, and in many cases, their interference is calculated and deliberate. Understanding these tactics helps you prepare for them and avoid costly setbacks. Some of the more common tactics include:

- **Questioning signature validity without cause**. Boards may compare petition signatures to past ballots, meeting sign-in sheets, or other documents and claim they "don't match." Legally, the correct process is to verify directly with the signer, not to reject signatures based on subjective comparisons.

- **Challenging the petition language**. Some boards will argue that the petition is "ambiguous" or "defective" because of minor word choices, formatting, or a lack of superfluous details.

- **Delaying the process**. Boards may slow-walk the 20-day notice requirement or set the meeting date outside the statutory 35–150 or 120–150 day window.

- **Arranging resignations to void the recall**. A targeted director may resign before the election so the board can appoint a replacement, potentially nullifying the petition and requiring petitioners to start over. Unfortunately, there's nothing that you can do to prevent this from happening...once. But if it happens again, you'll have strong grounds to challenge the replacement as a mere pretext to avoid an otherwise valid recall attempt, and courts don't look kindly on that sort of gamesmanship.

- **Ballot manipulation**. Some boards issue ballots that only ask whether to remove directors, without including the replacement election on the same ballot. If the removal passes but replacements aren't elected immediately, the board can fill vacancies with its own allies.

- **Restricting access to member contact information**. By refusing to provide mailing addresses or email lists, boards make it harder for petitioners to campaign, collect enough signatures, or inform owners of the facts before voting. Under Civil Code section 5200, you have a right to that information.

A recall is one of the most powerful tools California homeowners have to hold their HOA boards accountable, but only if it's done properly. The statutory requirements under both the Davis–Stirling Act and the Corporations Code are detailed and unforgiving, and boards that want to resist removal will often exploit any mistake to derail the process.

Success starts with a clear strategy. In most cases, recalling the entire board is more effective than targeting individual directors because most California HOAs have cumulative voting. From there, the process must be executed with precision, meaning that organizers must draft the petition properly, collect signatures only from eligible owners of record, and deliver the original petition signatures in a manner that cannot be disputed. Once the petition is in, the timelines for noticing and holding the meeting and mailing the ballots must be followed exactly, with special attention to whether cumulative voting or electronic voting applies in your association.

If done right, a recall can restore transparency, compliance, and accountability to your HOA.

Practical Strategies to Ensure Fair Elections

Watching for abuses and knowing how to challenge them is essential, but the best course of action is to prevent manipulation *before* it happens. Homeowners who take a few smart steps in advance can make it harder for a bad HOA board to control the process and easier to win fair outcomes. Simply put, with the right preparation, you can tilt the balance back toward fairness and accountability

- **Organize a voting bloc**. Elections are won by numbers, and entrenched HOA boards rely on voter apathy, knowing that only a small fraction of homeowners will return their ballots. If you and a group of neighbors commit to voting together, and you encourage others to do the same, you can quickly swing an election that might otherwise be decided by just a handful of ballots. Start by talking to neighbors you trust, sharing accurate information about what the law requires, and agreeing to remind each other to return ballots on time. Doing this won't take nearly as much time as you might think.

- **Use records requests strategically**. As we discussed a few chapters earlier, California law gives you the right to inspect association records, including membership lists and election materials. Use those rights. Ask for the membership list early so challengers can reach out to your fellow members—i.e., the voters. If the board resists, that resistance itself is a red flag you can later use to challenge the results. By making strategic records requests, you not only arm yourself with information but also send a signal that members are paying attention.

- **Coordinate with inspectors and observers**. Independent inspectors are required, but their job is easier, and a bad HOA will find it harder to cheat—when members make it clear that they're going to show up and that they're watching. Homeowners have the right to attend the ballot count. Coordinate with other members to be present when ballots are opened, confirm that envelopes are being handled correctly, and note anything suspicious. Truly independent inspectors are less likely to bend to board pressure when they know members are observing.

- **Run campaigns the right way**. You do not need glossy mailers or expensive consultants to run for the board. What matters is credibility and clarity. Stay focused on issues that affect everyone, like reserve funds concerns, maintenance lapses, or fairness in enforcement. Do not get sidetracked into personal attacks on current directors. Bad HOA board members thrive on framing challengers as "troublemakers." Stick to the facts, communicate respectfully, and emphasize your commitment to fairness and transparency. That tone will win more votes than anger ever will.

- **Build long-term credibility**. One election is important, but your reputation in the community matters even more. Boards come and go, but homeowners remember who communicates respectfully, who shares useful information, and who stands up for fairness without making it personal. By building credibility over time, you make it easier to organize voters, attract good candidates, and challenge misconduct when necessary. A board can dismiss one frustrated homeowner. It cannot dismiss a well-organized and well respected homeowners (or a group) who consistently speak with credibility and persistence.

Taken together, these moves can significantly shift the balance of power *before any wrongdoing has occurred*. Boards count on members staying silent, divided, or apathetic. When homeowners organize, act strategically, and stay focused on fairness, they not only level the playing field but also build lasting credibility that no board can ignore.

Challenging Election Results

When boards ignore the rules, you are not stuck with a rigged outcome. The Davis-Stirling Act gives homeowners a clear path to challenge unlawful elections and obtain real relief (Civ. Code, § 5145). This section of the law is unusually strong because it spells out clear grounds for action, a straightforward process, and meaningful remedies for homeowners.

Not every irregularity justifies a lawsuit, but many common abuses do. Among the more common election-related abuses that homeowners most often challenge include situations like these, where the board, its agents, or the inspector:

- Miss required notices or timelines.

- Disqualify legally eligible candidates.

- Break ballot secrecy by tying votes to names or addresses.

- Appoint inspectors who are not independent.

- Refuse to provide a membership list to challengers who request it for the purposes of campaigning.

- Fail to perform legally required, election-related duties.

- Mishandle ballots, fail to count them in public, or fail to safeguard them after the election.

- Allow directors to tap association funds, staff, or resources for their campaigns.

- Give incumbents access to HOA facilities, such as the clubhouse, while denying challengers equal access.

These abuses are not technicalities. Each one strikes at the heart of election fairness, and California courts can and do invalidate elections when they occur.

What Can Homeowners Do?

If you suspect election misconduct, start building your record immediately.

- Keep everything: ballots, envelopes, nomination forms, and election notices.

- Save emails or texts that show shifting deadlines, board interference, or campaign abuses.

- Request the written election rules and the membership list, and save proof of your requests.

- If the election has not yet occurred, put the board on notice and demand compliance before ballots go out.

- If the election has already taken place, demand that the results be set aside and the process redone correctly.

The point is simple: build a clean, chronological file. A strong paper trail turns suspicions into proof and strengthens your position if the dispute reaches court.

Just as important, keep emotion out of your communications. Stay professional, avoid personal attacks, and write as though a judge or jury will read every word—because they might. You want to always present your best case and appear credible and reasonable. Doing so will strengthen your position far more than you might think.

Remedies and Outcomes Under Civil Code Section 5145

If you bring an action under section 5145, the court has wide authority to correct the problem. In other words, when it comes to faulty elections, the Davis-Stirling Act has teeth. If you have to sue, the court can:

- Order the HOA to hold an election it refused to conduct. You might have a situation where the HOA has failed to set mandatory elections.

- Compel the board to comply with election procedures and statutory timelines.

- Invalidate unlawful results and require a new, fair election.

- Impose statutory penalties of up to $500 per proven violation. These can add up when bad HOAs breach multiple rules.

- Force the HOA to pay your attorney's fees and costs when you prevail.

With respect to the fee award, it favors the homeowners significantly because it's virtually one-way. If you win, the HOA pays your reasonable attorney's fees. If you lose, you only risk paying the HOA's fees if the court determines that your case was frivolous. That's an extremely high bar to reach, so the risk to you is very low. That structure is rare in HOA law, and it dramatically shifts the risk balance in favor of homeowners.

One more critical point: you must act quickly. Section 5145 gives you only *one year* from the date of the violation to bring your claim. Miss that deadline and your right to challenge the veracity of the election will disappear no matter how strong your evidence or violative the election process proved to be.

These remedies matter because they shift power back to homeowners. A board that ignores the rules is no longer in full control. And because the HOA can only recover its own fees if your case was frivolous or in bad faith, the law encourages legitimate claims rather than deterring them.

Last Thought on Board Elections

Board elections decide who controls your community's money, rules, and future. That makes them the single most important event in the life of an HOA. When run fairly, elections give homeowners a voice and a check on board power. When manipulated, they strip members of both.

This chapter has shown you what to watch for, how to organize, and what legal tools you have when the board crosses the line. The message is simple: you are not powerless. By preparing early, documenting carefully, and staying professional, you can protect your rights and safeguard your community's integrity. And if your board refuses to follow the law, California gives you the leverage to challenge them in court and win.

Fair elections are not a favor the board grants you. They are a right the law guarantees. Use that right.

Can My HOA Pass a Special Assessment Without a Member Vote?

Yes, but only under very limited circumstances.

Under Civil Code § 5605, HOAs can't impose special assessments exceeding 5% of the association's total annual budgeted expenses unless the assessment has been approved by a vote of a majority of the members. Not a board vote. A member vote.

And no, saying "we talked about it at a meeting" doesn't count. If your HOA's board failed to properly notice and conduct a proper membership vote, you'll be able challenge the assessment and stop collection entirely.

Now, there's one exception: emergencies. But even there, the law defines "emergencies" very narrowly. Legally valid emergencies include:

- Court-ordered repairs.
- Immediate threats to health and safety.
- Situations that require urgent action that couldn't have been reasonably foreseen.

To be clear, deferred maintenance, poor planning, or "we didn't budget for this" DO NOT qualify as emergencies. They qualify as mismanagement.

So, if your HOA hits your community with a special assessment in an amount over 5% of the annual budgeted expenses and there was no member vote or a *valid* emergency, then your HOA broke the law, and the special assessment will be declared invalid. You just have to challenge it.

ASSESSMENTS, MAINTENANCE, AND RESERVES

M ONEY IS THE engine that drives every HOA, and it comes directly from the pockets of homeowners. Your regular assessments—the monthly dues you pay—along with special assessments that you may have to pay from time to time are the primary sources of money used to fund everything that the board is obligated to do under the Davis-Stirling Act. That money pays for maintaining, repairing, and replacing the common areas, funding reserves for major future projects, and hiring the vendors needed to keep the community running. In short, money is one of the two primary sources from which HOA boards derive and exercise their power over homeowners (the other being the legal authority granted to boards under the Davis-Stirling Act).

This chapter is about how boards use, misuse, and sometimes abuse that financial power. We will focus on the rules for setting regular and special assessments, the board's legal duty to maintain the property, and the obligation to keep adequate reserves for major future repairs.

We are not talking here about fines for rule violations (covered in Chapter 6) or about insurance obligations (covered in Chapter 5). The focus here is on the recurring financial commitments every homeowner shares and what happens when boards fail to handle them responsibly.

The Ins and Outs of HOA Assessments

When you buy into an HOA, you agree to pay both regular assessments, which are typically due monthly, and special assessments, which are levied for specific projects or unexpected costs.

General assessments, or regular member dues, are the lifeblood of every HOA. Under the Davis-Stirling Act, assessments are not optional contributions. They are mandatory obligations tied to ownership of your property because the law requires associations to collect enough money to maintain, repair, and replace the common areas. Regular assessments cover the routine costs of running the day-to-day aspects of the community: landscaping, utilities for common areas, management fees, insurance premiums, and regular maintenance and repairs.

Special assessments, on the other hand, are imposed when the regular budget falls short, typically due to unforeseen repairs, true emergencies, or the board's failure to adequately fund reserves. In well-managed HOAs with properly maintained reserves, special assessments should be rare.

The amount each homeowner pays in terms of general and special assessments is, in most cases, a simple math formula where all the members pay an equal amount. This is sometimes referred to as a proportional or pro-rata share. In some developments, however, the CC&Rs alter this formula so that certain unit types (differentiated by type, square footage, or model), will pay more or less than a proportional share. If your HOA's CC&Rs don't specify how assessments should be calculated, then the default is that all members pay their proportional share.

While this may seem straightforward, the board's discretion in setting budgets and levying assessments is one of the most powerful tools it has. When used responsibly, it ensures the community is well-maintained and financially stable. When misused, it can create financial hardship, lead to unfair burdens on certain homeowners, or even push an association toward insolvency.

Legal Rules for Assessments

The Davis-Stirling Act gives boards broad authority to levy both regular and special assessments. In fact, the law goes further than that. The Davis-Stirling Act actually *requires* HOAs to assess its members in whatever amount is necessary to "sufficient[ly]...perform its obligations under the governing documents..." (Civ. Code, § 5600). *In other words, not only does the Davis-Stirling Act give your HOA broad authority to collect assessments from you, it actually requires them to do it.*

And yet, that statutory duty comes with important limits. Boards cannot exercise this power however they wish. They must follow strict procedures when increasing dues, imposing special assessments, and notifying members. Indeed, while HOA boards have broad discretion in setting their communities' regular assessments, the law restricts how much they can raise those general assessments on any given occasion without a member vote (Civ. Code, § 5605).

Under that provision of the Davis-Stirling Act, the board cannot increase regular assessments by more than 20% per year unless "a majority of a quorum of members" vote to approve the increase.[1] This restriction is designed to keep boards from plugging financial holes through sudden hikes, and it forces them to engage in real budgeting.

Special assessments are different. These are one-time charges levied for costs outside the annual budget, such as emergency repairs or unexpected expenses that couldn't reasonably be anticipated or budgeted for. The Davis-Stirling Act prohibits boards from imposing special assessments in excess of 5% of the HOA's budgeted gross expenses without

---

1. The distinction between a vote of the majority of members entitled to vote and a majority of a quorum of members can be significant. Suppose your HOA has 100 members. If the voting threshold for a particular election is a majority of members entitled to vote, then *at least 51 members would have to vote in favor* of whatever was up for election. But, if the threshold were a majority of a quorum of members, then an HOA with 100 members, would only need 26 votes in favor to succeed because a quorum would consist of 51, and 26 would constitute a majority of a quorum. That's a significant difference.

a majority vote of a quorum of the members (Civ. Code, § 5605).[2] For example, if your HOA's annual budget is $500,000, then your board couldn't pass a special assessment in excess of $25,000 without the required vote. And to be clear, the $25,000 is *not* $25,000 per member. It's $25,000 in total.

There are narrow statutory exceptions for true emergencies, such as complying with a court order, addressing immediate threats to health and safety, or making immediate repairs necessary to prevent significant damage to other property. But bad HOA boards often abuse these exceptions either because they don't want to bother with seeking member approval, or to cover up systemic failures on their part to perform regular maintenance and repairs until it was too late. Consequently, it isn't at all unusual for an HOA from Hell to declare an "emergency" where none exists.

Some really dishonest boards try to get around the member-vote requirement by breaking up a large project into smaller projects (and, so their thinking goes, smaller assessments). They believe that doing that absolves them of the 5% threshold. They are wrong. Neither of those is remotely legal, and homeowners can take action to stop such boards in their tracks. When challenged, such special assessments are almost certainly going to be declared void on their face.

When an HOA does increase assessments, the Davis-Stirling Act requires HOAs to provide between 30 and 60 days' notice to the members before the increased assessment goes into effect (Civ. Code, § 5615). This notice requirement applies to increases in both regular and special assessments.

If a board violates these rules, the assessment is not going to be legally enforceable. That means it will not be able to serve as the basis for a lien or foreclosure action, and it exposes the board to potential liability if they attempt to (or actually do) collect anyway. Homeowners

---

2. "[B]udgeted gross expenses includes reserve contributions. Had the statute said "budgeted operating expenses," then it would've excluded reserve contributions.

should be vigilant about these protections because bad HOA boards will often move forward with collection efforts until they are challenged.

The HOA's Duty to Maintain Common Areas

Assessments exist for a reason. They fund the board's duty to maintain, repair, and replace the common areas.

The Davis-Stirling Act imposes a mandatory legal duty on every HOA in the state to maintain, repair, and replace all common areas (Civ. Code, § 4775). *That duty is not contingent on budget availability, board discretion, or member approval.* Rather, that duty is among the most fundamental of an HOA's various obligations.[3] In practice, this means the board cannot simply decide to ignore deteriorating facilities, push costs back onto homeowners without legal authority, or let the property fall into disrepair.

In most multi-family HOAs (like condominiums and a lot of townhomes), what makes up the common area is broadly defined to almost always include things like roofs, exterior walls, plumbing lines, elevators, fences, parking areas, roads, greenbelts, and various recreational amenities, all of which then almost always fall under the board's responsibility.

Many governing documents also create "exclusive use common areas," such as balconies, patios, or garage doors, which are owned in common but designated for the exclusive use of a particular homeowner. In those cases, unless otherwise stated in the HOA's CC&Rs, the homeowner is responsible for *maintaining* their exclusive use common area, while the HOA is responsible for *repairing or replacing* those areas (Civ. Code, § 4775).

---

3. These default duties, such as a board's obligation to maintain, repair, and replace common areas, can be changed by provisions of an HOA's CC&Rs. But in almost all cases, such requirements remain with the board, so exceptions to that aren't worth discussing at this time.

And this is where many disputes begin. Bad HOA boards frequently attempt to dodge their statutory duty by redefining what counts as "common area." For example, a leaking roof or failing structural component may be mischaracterized as the responsibility of the individual homeowner, even when the governing documents list it as a common element that the HOA is solely responsible for maintaining, repairing, or replacing. Other boards defer necessary repairs year after year, claiming lack of funds or waiting for a crisis to force action. Both of those "strategies" not only violate the law, they also undermine property values and put homeowners at financial and personal risk.

A neglected plumbing system, for example, may cause water damage in multiple units. If the board refuses to take responsibility, homeowners can be left fighting expensive battles to prove that the association, not them, is responsible for the repairs. Bad HOA boards will frequently play the game of denying responsibility for maintenance and repairs of assets that they know full well are their responsibility until confronted with their own governing documents, Civil Code section 4775, and the threat of litigation by a member.

The connection between maintenance and money cannot be overstated. Regular assessments are supposed to cover the day-to-day costs of upkeep, while reserves are intended to fund future replacements or reasonably foreseeable but infrequent costs that arise from time to time. When boards underfund or mismanage these resources, they often cut corners on maintenance or attempt to shift costs to homeowners.

This not only erodes trust but also exposes the association to liability and the members to financial hardship. Recognizing when your HOA is shirking its obligations, and knowing how to challenge those failures, gives homeowners leverage to hold their boards accountable.[4]

---

4. The how-to of holding your HOA accountable comes later in the book, where we walk through the specific tools available to homeowners to enforce these duties.

Understanding HOA Reserves

As we discussed in Chapter 5, the Davis-Stirling Act requires HOAs to prepare and disclose reserve studies so that members can determine whether the association has financially prepared for future repairs and replacements of the association's major components. Reserve studies provide the technical side of this obligation, consisting of the spreadsheets, projections, and disclosures that boards must update and share. But reserves do more than just satisfy a legal requirement on paper. They stand as one of the three pillars of HOA financial power, along with assessments and maintenance.

Reserves exist for a simple reason: to prepare for the inevitable. The two things that all of your HOA's major components have in common with each other are that they all require periodic maintenance, and they will all eventually fail and need to be replaced. That is a scientific certainty. Roofs, along with all other major components like roads, elevators, recreational facilities, and structures, eventually require replacement.

Without properly funded reserves, HOAs fall into crisis management, relying on sudden special assessments or loans that blindside homeowners. In other words, the entire purpose of HOA reserves is to insulate members from financial shocks. When boards ignore or underfund reserves, HOA members *always* pay the price. Unfortunately, bad HOA boards routinely mishandle reserves. Some underfund them year after year to keep regular assessments artificially low, passing the true cost of long-term maintenance and replacements onto future HOA members... sort of a bury your head in the sand approach. Others raid reserve accounts to cover operating shortfalls caused by systemic negligence, leaving nothing for major replacements. Still others manipulate reserve components to distort the all-important "percent funded" number discussed in Chapter 5.

Each of these practices drive the community toward financial instability, resulting in very real and very severe financial consequences. Homeowners in drastically underfunded associations often face periodic massive special assessments, sometimes tens of thousands of dollars per household, when one or more major projects simply cannot be delayed any longer. Likewise, mortgage lenders and insurers scrutinize reserve funding closely. An association that reports reserves at only 20%, 30%, or 40% of recommended levels signals financial risk. That drives up insurance premiums, limits or temporarily eliminates financing options for buyers, and depresses property values.

Reserves, then, are not a luxury or a technicality. They show whether an HOA operates responsibly or recklessly. They reveal whether the board plans for the community's future or pushes problems onto the next generation of owners. Assessments may keep the lights on and maintenance may keep the property standing, but adequate reserves keep the association stable.

Your HOA Can Regulate Your Remodel, But the Rules Must Be Reasonable

Almost all HOAs in California have the power to regulate what you build or modify on your property. But that power isn't unlimited.

Under Civil Code § 4765, your HOA can't deny your remodel, landscaping, or exterior improvement request based on vague aesthetic preferences or personal opinion. Any denial must be based on a published standard in the governing documents. And most importantly, the rules enforced by your HOA must be reasonable, and NOT arbitrary, capricious, or inconsistent with prior approvals.

Now, in certain specific situations, the law has curtailed your HOA's ability to regulate the existence or scope of your improvements. For example, HOAs cannot prevent homeowners from installing satellite dishes, solar panels, EV charging stations, drought-resistant landscaping, or Accessory Dwelling Units. Nor can the HOA prevent a disabled individual from installing improvements that would qualify as reasonable accommodations under federal and state housing laws.

Regardless, in the case of a denial, the Davis-Stirling Act also requires a timely, written decision that clearly explains the reasons for denial. If your board is dragging its feet, moving the goalposts, or making up rules as they go, they're not just overstepping, they're likely violating the law.

ARCHITECTURAL CONTROL AND PROPERTY RESTRICTIONS

F EW AREAS OF HOA law create more conflict for California home-owners than architectural control. Most HOA boards are empow-ered to assert broad authority over how members may use and improve their own property, governing everything from the addition of an acces-sory dwelling unit (ADU) to repainting a home, planting/replacing land-scaping, adding an extra room, or installing solar panels. HOAs justify these restrictions in the name of "community character" or "aesthetic harmony," something which the Davis-Stirling Act empowers them to do under a concept from corporate law called the business judgment rule (BJR). But that power is far from unlimited.

Civil Code section 4765 requires every HOA architectural decision to be reasonable, made in good faith, and based on published stan-dards in the governing documents. If a board relies on "guidelines" that were never adopted as operating rules in compliance with Civil Code sections 4350–4360 (including notice to members and an opportunity to comment), those restrictions are legally vulnerable. A board cannot enforce unwritten preferences or rules that were never lawfully adopted. They must also be applied uniformly. Boards cannot invent new require-ments mid-process, delay decisions indefinitely, issue denials based solely on subjective preferences, or treat some homeowners differently than others.

Other California statutes go even further. For example, Civil Code section 4751 protects a homeowner's right to construct an ADU, Civil Code section 4735 protects a homeowner's right to plant drought-re-sistant landscaping, and Civil Code sections 714–714.1 safeguard a homeowner's right to install a solar power system. Laws like those form a legal framework that curbs HOA overreach and secures homeowners' rights to improve their property.

When properly enforced, architectural control helps maintain community safety, design consistency, and property values. When abused, which happens all too frequently, such control becomes a weapon to delay projects, retaliate against outspoken members, or manipulate the community's appearance according to the personal preferences of those in power.

Where do HOAs Get Their Architectural Authority?

HOAs do not automatically have the power to control what homeowners can build, paint, or plant on their own properties. That authority has to come from the governing documents. In most communities, the CC&Rs contain provisions that give the board, or an appointed architectural committee, the power to review and approve homeowner projects. Sometimes the CC&Rs are explicit and list the kinds of changes that require approval. Other times the language is broad, giving the board authority to adopt more specific Rules or Architectural Guidelines that fill in the details.

Either way, the Davis-Stirling Act imposes real limits on how that authority may be exercised. Even when an HOA's CC&Rs give the board power to regulate architectural changes, that power must be consistent with the various provisions of the Davis–Stirling Act that address property improvements. Civil Code section 4350, for example, controls the adoption of Rules, and Civil Code section 4765 sets out the standards for architectural review. That statute also sharply limits the protection of the BJR by requiring architectural decisions to be grounded in actual written standards, made in good faith, and applied consistently.

In short, the law requires that architectural standards be:

- Specifically set forth in the governing documents, or if later adopted, they must be adopted properly, with required notice, and an opportunity for homeowner input.

- Clear and consistent with higher-ranking governing documents.

- Reasonable, made in good faith, and applied uniformly.

If an HOA board can't point to either explicit authority in the CC&Rs or properly adopted Rules or Architectural Guidelines, then it doesn't have a legal basis to deny a member's plans. Unfortunately, many homeowners don't realize that architectural control is one of the board's most commonly abused powers. Boards often use vague phrases like "community harmony" or "aesthetic standards" to justify arbitrary decisions. But unless those standards are written in the governing documents, and adopted lawfully, they carry no weight. Knowing where the board's authority comes from, and where it doesn't, is the first step in pushing back against improper denials.

How the Law Limits HOA Power Over Architectural Decisions

The Davis–Stirling Act does not give HOA boards unlimited authority to dictate how homeowners improve their property. Civil Code section 4765 sets strict standards for architectural review, and when boards ignore those requirements, their decisions are legally vulnerable. Under section 4765, all architectural decisions must be made in good faith and may *not* be:

- **Unreasonable.** A denial must make sense in light of the facts and the governing documents. A rejection that contradicts past approvals, lacks justification in the Rules, or ignores the actual standards in place is likely going to be deemed unenforceable.

- **Arbitrary**. Standards must be applied uniformly and rationally. A decision is arbitrary when it lacks a reasonable basis, is not grounded in the governing documents, or ignores objective standards. It reflects action taken without reference to rules, facts, or established criteria. It's essentially a decision "made up" without justification. For example, a homeowner applies to install a backyard patio cover. The HOA's architectural guidelines clearly allow patio covers of neutral colors. The board denies the request simply because they personally don't like this particular homeowner or because a few board members think that patio covers "look tacky," even though the written standards permit it. The denial has no tie to the rules, and is thus arbitrary.

- **Capricious**. A decision is capricious when it is inconsistent, unpredictable, or based on sudden whim rather than steady application of standards. If a board approves your project one month and reverses itself the next without justification, that's capricious and illegal.

Section 4765 also imposes process requirements:

- **Boards must act fairly and expeditiously**. They cannot sit on your application indefinitely or invent hurdles that don't appear in the governing documents.

- **Decisions must be in writing**. Verbal approvals or casual emails are not legally valid.

- **Denials must state reasons**. A board cannot simply stamp "denied" on your application. It must explain the basis, citing specific Rules or CC&R provisions. Indeed, a compliant written decision should identify the specific governing-document provision or properly adopted rule being applied, the facts the board relied on, and the steps required (if any) for you to obtain approval. When a decision lacks those elements, it becomes far easier to challenge as arbitrary, unreasonable, or out of step with Civil Code section 4765.

Some CC&Rs also contain "auto-approval" provisions stating that if the board fails to respond within a set timeframe (e.g., within 30–45 days), the plans are deemed approved. When that deadline passes without action, a homeowner has the legal right to proceed.

But even if your HOA's governing documents do not contain such auto-approval language, your board cannot evade deadlines by announcing a "temporary pause" or a de facto moratorium while they rethink guidelines or attempt to pass new rules aimed at your specific application. Unless the governing documents lawfully authorize a pause, applications must be processed under existing standards and within the published timelines. An HOA that stalls to avoid a timely yes-or-no decision risks having the court step in on the homeowner's side for failure to act fairly and expeditiously.

Even with all of the above-referenced limitations in place, HOA boards from Hell routinely overstep as a means of asserting illegal control over homeowner decisions. The most common signs that your board is overstepping include denials based on vague phrases like "not harmonious," requirements that aren't written anywhere in the governing documents, or patterns of selective enforcement. These are red flags that the board is misusing its power. Recognizing these warning signs early can help you document abuses and build a stronger case if you need to challenge the decision.

Examples of Common Board Abuses Regarding Architectural Review

Even with clear legal limits in place, HOAs from Hell stretch or ignore those limits when reviewing architectural applications. Homeowners need to know what these abuses look like in practice so that they can recognize them quickly and push back. The most common red flags include:

- **Vague aesthetic language**. Denials based on phrases like "not harmonious" or "doesn't fit the character of the neighborhood" are, absent additional details, almost always suspect. Without specific standards in the CC&Rs, Rules, or Architectural Guidelines, these phrases carry no legal meaning.

- **Restrictions not stated in the governing documents**. Boards sometimes reject projects by citing rules that don't actually exist in any governing document. HOAs cannot enforce standards that were never adopted properly, or don't exist in any governing document. If they can't point to it in writing, they can't enforce it.

- **Selective enforcement**. When one homeowner's project is denied for violating a rule that other neighbors have clearly violated without consequence, the board is engaging in illegal selective enforcement. Rules must be applied uniformly.

- **Retaliation against critics**. Some boards use the architectural process as a weapon against homeowners who have opposed them in elections, challenged them in meetings, or spoken out publicly. A project that meets all published standards but is denied anyway can be a sign of retaliation, which is not only abusive but unlawful as well.

- **Requiring preferred contractors**. HOAs cannot legally deny an application just because the owner did not hire the HOA's preferred contractor. Nor can boards require any homeowner to hire a specified contractor to make repairs on the member's property (unless the HOA is paying for the work).

These abuses aren't minor technicalities. They go to the heart of Civil Code section 4765, which requires fairness, good faith, and uniform application of standards.

You should document every step of the application process. Save copies of your plans, communications, and especially the board's written decision. If a denial lacks detail, cites vague language, or points to rules you've never seen, those are immediate red flags that the decision may not be enforceable.

Bad Faith Tactics to Delay Applications

Some bad HOAs know that they won't get away with denying a request outright, so they will often rely on delay as a weapon instead. Rather than saying no, they try to wear homeowners down with endless "reviews," shifting requirements, or engaging in sabotage after approval. Common delay tactics include:

- **Submission purgatory**. The board refuses to give a clear yes or no, instead demanding "clarifications" or "additional plans" again and again. This tactic is designed to stall indefinitely without triggering the statutory protections for formal denials.

- **Post-approval sabotage**. A homeowner gets written approval, starts construction, and then the board changes its mind, claiming that the work "doesn't match" the approved plans or that "new information" requires reversal. Unless the project has materially deviated from what was approved, this tactic is unlawful, and can be ignored.[1]

- **Shifting standards**. The application complies with every published requirement, but the board suddenly "reinterprets" the guidelines or applies new ones retroactively.

---

1. As a matter of caution, just know that taking such an admittedly aggressive stance could cause the HOA to file legal action against the homeowner. That being said, the HOA would be foolish to do that if in fact it was really playing games, so this is often a good litmus test to determine whether the HOA is confident in its claims, or if they know that their demands are bogus.

- **Moving goalposts**. The board denies the request, but tells the homeowner what to change to get approval. After the homeowner makes those changes, the board invents new objections never mentioned in an earlier denial.

Such tactics are common amongst bad HOA boards, and they undermine the protections of Civil Code section 4765. Architectural review is not supposed to be a game of attrition. If your board is dragging things out or constantly changing the rules, it's not exercising legitimate discretion, and it's therefore violating the law.

Statutory Carve-Outs Limiting HOA Architectural Control

Civil Code section 4765 provides the general standards for HOA architectural review. But beyond those general requirements, the Legislature has enacted additional statutes that address specific areas where HOAs often try to overreach, such as ADUs (sometimes called "granny flats"), drought-resistant landscaping, and solar energy systems. I discuss some of those in greater detail below.

Accessory Dwelling Units (ADUs)

Although most of the statutory protections have been in place for years, I'm sometimes caught off guard to see the ways in which bad HOA boards continue to abuse their authority in subtle but persistent ways.

ADUs, sometimes referred to as "granny flats," "accessory apartments," or "in-law units," are now a permanent fixture in California housing policy. But for many homeowners living in HOA-governed communities, the legal path to building one still feels uncertain despite the powerful public policy supporting California's ADU laws. *To be sure, state law severely limits what HOAs can do to block or delay ADU construction, but that hasn't stopped many boards from trying.*

Under current California law, the answer to whether an HOA can deny an ADU is almost always no. In most cases, a California HOA cannot legally prohibit a homeowner from building an ADU on their property. The state's ADU laws, which were recently reorganized and expanded, make it illegal for homeowners' associations to adopt or enforce rules that unreasonably restrict the construction or use of an ADU or Junior ADU (sometimes called a JADU).

This means that even if your HOA's CC&Rs include language that appears to prohibit detached structures, such as "granny flats," "accessory apartments," or any other euphemism for an ADU, those provisions are unenforceable because they directly conflict with state law. And if your HOA is refusing to approve your plans outright, or demanding that you "apply for a variance" just to consider your request, that is a major red flag because what they're doing is completely illegal.

It is true that HOAs retain *limited* authority to impose reasonable design restrictions, like architectural uniformity or utility safety compliance, on ADUs. But that's about it. They cannot flatly deny ADUs, impose ADU-specific costs or fees, make up new hurdles to jump through, or take any steps to make construction impracticable just because the board or architectural committee does not want them in the community.

California's ADU laws are not vague. The Legislature has made it explicitly clear that homeowners in single-family residential zones have the right to build ADUs and JADUs on their property, regardless of whether the home is located inside a common interest development. In fact, the new law, AB 130, amended Civil Code section 714.3 to make that even more clear than it was before. HOAs cannot override or ignore the law by citing outdated CC&Rs, manufactured approval processes, or relying on aesthetic objections.

Boards also cannot use "variance" demands or bespoke conditions to sidestep the Davis-Stirling Act's ADU protections (Civ. Code, § 4751). If your ADU meets state and local requirements and any truly reasonable design standards (e.g., materials to match the primary residence, utility safety), the HOA must process the application without delay. Requiring additional hurdles that do not apply to ordinary construction, or conditioning approval on discretionary "character" findings, is exactly the kind of unreasonable restriction the law prohibits the HOA from engaging in.

Simply put, if your ADU complies with state and local law, your HOA cannot legally stop you from building it, nor can it impose or enforce any requirement that unreasonably restricts the construction or use of an ADU or JADU (Civ. Code, § 4751).[2] So, while HOAs can adopt reasonable standards related to design and placement, they may not ban ADUs entirely, nor may they impose arbitrary rules designed to obstruct the process.

For example, an HOA might be permitted to require that your ADU's exterior materials match your primary residence or that utility hookups meet safety standards. But it cannot do things like:

- Ban ADUs outright.

- Impose additional parking requirements beyond what the local government requires.

- Refuse to review your application based on "neighborhood character" or aesthetics.

- Demand setbacks or height restrictions beyond those found in local zoning law.

- Impose ADU-related fees or costs (i.e., costs that don't apply to all construction).

---

2. Although not explicitly applicable to HOAs, many experts, including myself, argue that because HOAs act as quasi-governmental entities, they should be held to the same standards as those set forth in Government Code section 66317, which applies to governmental entities, and imposes timelines and restrictions relating to the approval of ADUs.

- Require additional materials as part of the application process (e.g., impact or environmental reports).

- Require your neighbors to sign off on your ADU plans.

- Delay approvals indefinitely or refuse to timely process your ADU plans.

California's public policies concerning ADUs supersede any controls that HOAs may wish to impose. Consequently, bad HOAs that continue to attempt to sidestep California's ADU laws or manipulate their own internal rules or approval processes to create barriers to ADU construction are exposing themselves to significant legal liability.

Drought-Resistant Landscaping

The Davis-Stirling Act explicitly protects the rights of California homeowners to install drought-resistant landscaping (Civ. Code, § 4735). But far too many bad HOAs either don't know that or don't care. And while the law was designed to curb aesthetic overreach and support responsible water use, bad HOA boards continue to violate the law by blocking homeowners from planting drought-resistant landscaping, or by trying to pressure homeowners to remove already-approved grass, flowers, or shrubs in favor of drought-resistant fauna. And when state-mandated water restrictions hit, the confusion only gets worse.

This confusion doesn't just come from rogue boards. Many HOAs rely on outdated governing documents (passed prior to the passage of Civil Code § 4735), and many HOA boards rely on ignorant managers who don't understand the law. The statute itself, however, draws a bright line: *HOAs can't prohibit water-efficient landscaping based on aesthetics.* But enforcement remains wildly inconsistent, and most homeowners don't realize how much legal protection they actually have.

To be sure, the statute doesn't merely "encourage" water-wise design. It explicitly prohibits HOAs from banning it based on aesthetic grounds.

This is a massive departure from the powers granted to HOAs in their governing documents and in other parts of the Davis-Stirling Act, where the BJR normally grants HOA boards broad discretion over aesthetics. Indeed, under Civil Code section 4735, California HOAs cannot:

- **Prohibit low-water landscaping choices**. That includes planting native or water-wise species, artificial turf, or using gravel or bark, and it applies even if the new landscaping changes the visual appearance of a member's yard.

- **Fine a homeowner for letting the lawn die during a declared drought emergency**. If a state or local mandate restricts watering, and a member's lawn turns brown, the HOA can't penalize the member for complying with that mandate.

- **Require a member to undo drought-resistant changes after the emergency ends**. If a member replaced their lawn or installed hardscape features during a drought, the HOA has no legal right to demand that the member reverse those improvements once watering restrictions are lifted.

Those protections apply even if a member's neighbors complain or an owner's board dislikes the appearance of the drought-resistant landscaping. *The law prioritizes water conservation over uniform aesthetics.* That doesn't mean homeowners can plant anything, anywhere, without permission. HOAs can still require architectural approval for visible changes. But they cannot flatly deny a proposal just because they don't like the look of succulents, gravel, or artificial turf.

Civil Code section 4735 also bars HOAs from punishing homeowners for complying with state or local water restrictions. If the state or city limits irrigation, an HOA can't fine a member for having brown or dying grass.

Solar Energy Systems

More and more California homeowners are choosing to install solar systems. With utility rates climbing, rebate programs still available in some markets, and long-term savings nearly guaranteed, solar is no longer just about the environment, it's about economics. But what happens when an HOA says no? Or, as is often the case, when an HOA tries to impose unreasonable restrictions on a homeowner's solar power plans?

California law strongly favors solar access. Civil Code sections 714, 714.1, and 4746 work together to prohibit HOAs from adopting or enforcing any covenant, restriction, condition, or rule that "effectively prohibits or restricts" the installation of a solar energy system. The statute doesn't just outlaw outright bans, it also covers indirect restrictions that make a system unreasonably difficult, costly, or inefficient.

Under Civil Code section 714, an HOA may only impose restrictions on owners of single-family homes (or townhomes where owners own their roofs) if those restrictions:

- Do not increase the total cost of the system by more than $1,000.

- Do not reduce the system's expected electricity output by more than 10% (as measured in kilowatt hours).

Any restriction that exceeds either threshold is presumed unreasonable and therefore unenforceable. End of story.

HOA boards also face strict timelines. An HOA has 45 calendar days to approve or deny a solar application, or the application is automatically deemed approved. That rule ensures that silence cannot be used as a backdoor denial.

For condominiums where roofs are common area, Civil Code section 4746 allows individual owners to install solar energy systems on their pro-rata portion of the roof or parking space, provided certain conditions are met. HOAs may require such condo owners to carry insurance, enter into covenants accepting responsibility for maintenance and damage, and ensure that one installation does not interfere with another. But unless those conditions are clearly triggered, HOAs cannot use common area ownership to prohibit solar installations entirely. That is a drastic departure from the powers HOAs typically have over use of the common area.

And yet, despite the fact that the law on this subject is clear, many HOAs still try to work around it. Common tactics include:

- Pretending that Civil Code section 714 doesn't exist and imposing restrictions that reduce output by more than 10% or increase costs by more than $1,000.

- Delaying approvals beyond the statutory 45-day window.

- Denying applications without stating a clear reason in writing.

- Imposing reasonable conditions that aren't spelled out in the governing documents.

For homeowners, the practical lesson is that solar applications carry some of the strongest statutory protections offered under California law. If the board misses deadlines, demands expensive aesthetic changes, or reduces system efficiency beyond the statutory threshold, those actions are legally unenforceable.

Other Areas of Increased Legal Protections

The protections surrounding ADUs, drought-resistant landscaping, and solar energy systems represent the most litigated and highly developed carve-outs available under California law. The Legislature has recognized that HOAs are often most aggressive when policing major changes to homes and yards, and so it has created specific statutory protections to level the playing field for homeowners.

But those three items are not the only areas where state or federal law limits an HOA's power. Several additional carve-outs exist, each narrower in scope, but still important for homeowners to know. These protections may not warrant the same depth of treatment as ADUs, drought-resistant landscaping, or solar systems, but they are significant enough that every homeowner should at least be aware of them. The more significant examples include the following:

- **Electric Vehicle Charging Stations ("EVCS") [Civ. Code, §§ 4745–4745.1]**. HOAs cannot unreasonably restrict installation of EV charging stations in an owner's exclusive-use parking space. They may impose reasonable safety and indemnity requirements, but they cannot flatly ban EVCS.

- **Flags and Non-commercial Signs [Civ. Code, §§ 4705, 4710]**. Homeowners have the right to display the U.S. flag and certain non-commercial signs, posters, and banners. HOAs may regulate size, or placement for safety or maintenance reasons, but they cannot prohibit them outright on aesthetic grounds.

- **Security Cameras and Safety Devices**. Under Penal Code section 647(j), people have the right to privacy in places where they have a reasonable expectation of privacy. At the same time, homeowners have the right to protect themselves and their families. Despite what many HOA-side attorneys might claim (and they claim that HOAs have the right to impose rules banning all security cameras), I believe that HOAs have no power to prevent a homeowner from installing video (*not audio*) surveillance devices on *the homeowner's* property (or on property set aside for their exclusive use) provided that the cameras are not pointed into a neighbor's yard or home (and that such installation doesn't violate any other applicable reasonable restrictions). In other words, HOA boards may impose rules on whether recording devices may be installed in common areas (such as a doorbell in a condominium where the wall is common area), and they may require compliance with California's privacy laws. But I don't believe that any HOA would get away with imposing a blanket ban on security cameras on a member's private property or exclusive-use areas like a porch or balcony.

- **Satellite Dishes and Antennas [Civ. Code, § 4725; FCC OTARD Rule, 47 C.F.R. § 1.4000].** Although the Davis-Stirling Act explicitly references satellite dishes (Civ. Code, § 4725), it's irrelevant because federal law preempts California's state laws on the subject. Under federal law, HOAs cannot ban satellite dishes and antennas in areas exclusively controlled by the owner if restrictions would impair signal quality, increase cost, or delay installation. HOAs can, however, impose reasonable restrictions aimed at protecting public safety. HOAs can also require members to indemnify the HOA for repairs or maintenance if, for example, the satellite dishes or antennas are installed on common area components (e.g., roofs). Finally, while HOAs can require *prior notice* of a homeowner's installation of a satellite dish or antenna, they cannot require *prior approval* unless the equipment is being installed on non-exclusive use common area.

- **Clotheslines and Drying Racks [Civil Code § 4753].** HOAs cannot prohibit the use of clotheslines or drying racks in an owner's backyard. Reasonable rules are permitted, but flat bans are unenforceable.

- **Roofing Materials (Fire-Safe and Cool Roofs) [Civil Code § 4720; Health & Safety Code § 13132.7].** HOAs cannot ban fire-retardant or energy-efficient "cool roof" materials that comply with state safety and energy laws. Boards cannot force members to choose aesthetics over safety.

These carve-outs may seem narrow when compared to the broad authority boards typically enjoy under the BJR, but they demonstrate an important truth. When the Legislature identifies areas where HOA power too often leads to abuse, sometimes it intervenes. Whether it is protecting the right to build an ADU, conserve water, install a solar system, or embrace new technologies like electric vehicle charging, state and federal law sometimes set boundaries that HOA boards cannot cross.

For homeowners, the lesson is clear. Architectural authority is not unlimited, and when the statutes speak directly, those protections give members some of the strongest leverage available to push back against HOA overreach.

Practical Strategies for Homeowners

Understanding the law is only the first step. To make that knowledge useful, homeowners need clear strategies for navigating architectural approvals and fighting back when boards cross the line. The following practices can help members protect their rights and strengthen their position if disputes arise:

- **Get everything in writing**. Never rely on verbal approvals or casual conversations with board members or managers. Always insist on a written decision, and save all correspondence, applications, and notices. A complete paper trail is your best protection.

- **Demand specific reasons for denial**. Civil Code section 4765 requires the board to provide written reasons for any denial. If the board provides only vague phrases like "not harmonious," push back and require that they cite specific provisions from the governing documents.

- **Mark your calendar**. Many governing documents include "auto-approval" provisions if the board fails to act within a certain time frame (e.g., 30–45 days). If the deadline passes without a decision, homeowners may gain the right to proceed regardless of whether the plans violate the governing documents.

Even if no auto-approval clause exists, tracking timelines will help show if the board is stalling, which is itself illegal.

- **Compare past approvals.** If a board denies a request that is similar to projects it has previously approved, that is a red flag for selective enforcement. Document those comparisons with photos and/or videos whenever possible. Selective enforcement is illegal.

- **Challenge unwritten rules.** A board cannot invent restrictions on the fly. If a requirement does not appear in the governing documents, it is likely not enforceable. Always ask the board to cite its authority.

- **Stay professional.** Frustration is natural when a board abuses its power, but every letter or email should be written as though a judge or jury may one day read it. Remaining calm and factual builds credibility and avoids giving the board ammunition to paint the homeowner as unreasonable or unhinged.

- **Use dispute resolution strategically.** Homeowners can request IDR as a free, informal way to meet with the board. While not always effective, a well-prepared IDR session can force the board to explain its position and create useful documentation.

- **Know when to escalate.** If the board refuses to comply with the law or continues to obstruct, consult with an attorney with expertise in the Davis-Stirling Act (such as my law firm, MBK Chapman). Many statutes include fee-shifting provisions that allow homeowners to recover attorney's fees if they prevail, making enforcement more realistic.

By combining these practices with the statutory protections already discussed, homeowners can push back against arbitrary, unreasonable, or capricious architectural control and hold their boards accountable.

CAN YOU RECOVER YOUR ATTORNEY'S FEES AND COSTS IF YOU SUE YOUR HOA?

Yes, under Civil Code § 5975(c), homeowners can recover attorney's fees in California HOA lawsuits when they prevail in an enforcement action.

California follows the "American Rule," which allows recovery of attorney's fees only if a statute or contract provides for it. HOA CC&Rs are treated as binding contracts, and most include provisions awarding attorney's fees to the prevailing party. In addition, the Davis-Stirling Act explicitly awards the prevailing party its attorney's fees and costs in lawsuits related to the enforcement of the HOA's governing documents.

To understand the law, you have to understand two phrases: "prevailing party" and "enforcement action." Courts decide who the "prevailing party" is by looking at which side achieved its main litigation objectives, not just who technically "won" (e.g., obtained a verdict). "Enforcement actions" under the Davis–Stirling Act are broadly interpreted and can include lawsuits over: (a) requiring an HOA to maintain common areas; (b) challenging unfair or inconsistent board decisions; (c) stopping board misuse of HOA funds; or (c) forcing compliance with CC&Rs, rules, or required procedures.

Attorney's fees also include fees incurred during pre-lawsuit ADR in cases where the ADR was mandatory under Civil Code § 5930. Bottom line? If you sue your HOA, and if your lawsuit constitutes an enforcement action, then yes, you are entitled to an award of your attorney's fees and costs when you win.

HOA LITIGATION
AND ENFORCEMENT
IN CALIFORNIA

M OST HOA DISPUTES in California can be resolved without ever stepping foot in a courtroom. The Davis-Stirling Act gives homeowners the right to demand (and requires) that their HOAs engage in IDR. Likewise, in many cases, the Davis-Stirling Act requires HOAs and members in disputes with each other to engage in ADR before initiating litigation. You can review the details of those requirements in Chapter 7.

This chapter explains how enforcement actually works once a case reaches the courts. We will cover what types of disputes lend themselves to litigation, how penalties and attorney fees are awarded, and why both sides often underestimate the cost and risk of a full-blown lawsuit. You will also learn what options exist outside the traditional lawsuit process, such as seeking injunctive relief or filing a writ petition, and why those options can sometimes achieve faster results.

Above all, this chapter will give you a realistic picture of what it means to "take your HOA to court." Lawsuits can be powerful tools, but they are also blunt instruments. Knowing when litigation makes sense, and when it doesn't, is the key to protecting your rights without bankrupting yourself.

What is Litigation?

"Litigation" is an interesting word because it means different things in different contexts. For example, it can be used to describe a specific event, such as a trial or arbitration, or it can be used to describe an entire process, such as what occurs from the time a lawsuit or demand for arbitration is commenced all the way through an appeal.

For our purposes, litigation means the entire process. It starts the moment a lawsuit is filed and it can continue for months or even years.[1] While no two cases unfold in exactly the same way, most follow a familiar path that includes the following stages:

- **Filing the Case**. Litigation begins when someone files a complaint in court. The HOA may be the one suing, or the homeowner may be the one filing the case. The other side (the defendant) then files a response, which may admit, deny, or try to knock out some or all of the plaintiff's claims.

- **Information Gathering (Discovery)**. Once the case is underway, each side has the right to gather evidence. This process, called discovery, might include a combination of written questions, requests for documents and admissions, and depositions. All of those discovery tools are done under oath, which is why discovery can make or break a case. Discovery usually lasts the longest and can be extremely expensive.

- **Motions**. Along the way, either side may ask the court to decide key issues before trial. For example, a motion might seek to throw out part of the case, force the other side to hand over documents, or stop certain conduct through an injunction. These interim rulings can drastically shape how the case proceeds.

- **Trial Preparation and Trial**. If the case doesn't settle, both sides must at some point prepare for trial. That means organizing and marshaling evidence, lining up witnesses, and crafting arguments. Trials themselves can last from a few days to over

---

1. Some HOAs have binding arbitration provisions that require the parties to litigate disputes in private arbitration rather than state court. For the purposes of this book, however, we're disregarding such provisions and instead focusing on state court actions because the majority of CC&Rs do not contain binding arbitration provisions.

a month, depending on the complexity of the dispute. Most HOA-related trials can be concluded in a few days, although some do take a week or two.

- **Post-Trial and Appeals**. Even after trial, the case isn't necessarily over. Either side may file a variety of post-trial motions or even appeal the judgment to a higher court, prolonging the fight and increasing the costs.

For homeowners, the important takeaway is not how to navigate every procedural step. That's between you and your litigation attorney. Rather, it's to understand that litigation is a long, layered, and complex process. Each stage adds cost, stress, and risk. HOAs often bank on these pressures to wear down homeowners, hoping members will abandon valid claims simply because the process is so demanding and expensive.

Deciding Whether Litigation Makes Sense

Litigation is not the first step in an HOA dispute, but it is the most powerful tool *when all else fails*. For the reasons discussed in Chapter 7, homeowners should typically start with ADR, regardless of whether it's technically required or not under the Davis-Stirling Act. Remember, ADR is not only much faster than litigation, but it's far less costly, and homeowners can often negotiate concessions that would otherwise be unavailable in litigation. But when ADR does not resolve the problem, the question becomes whether a lawsuit is viable.

This is where working with an experienced attorney, like those at my firm, MBK Chapman, makes all the difference. An experienced HOA attorney will evaluate the specific facts of your case in terms of the applicable law to determine if there are causes of action strong enough to move forward with litigation. Some cases that made for excellent pre-litigation cases may not be good cases to actually bring to litigation. Other cases are ripe for litigation, and just take a decision by the homeowner to proceed.

If the case is viable, the homeowner essentially faces three options: (1) file a lawsuit and pursue the case, with the knowledge that if they prevail the HOA can be forced to pay their attorney's fees; (2) do nothing and accept the status quo; or (3) sell the property and walk away. For most homeowners who refuse to be bullied or ignored, in those cases where living with the status quo or selling their homes is not acceptable, litigation is the only option that truly corrects the abuse.

While every lawsuit carries some level of risk, the reward of court-ordered compliance and fee recovery often makes the decision clear. Litigation may be challenging, but in the absence of a favorable pre-litigation resolution, it is also the only path that can transform homeowner frustration into enforceable accountability.

Once a homeowner, in concert with his or her attorney, makes the decision to litigate, the focus shifts to strategy. Homeowners need to understand that litigation is not a single event but a series of stages—e.g., filing the complaint, gathering evidence through discovery, addressing motions, and, if necessary, going to trial. Each stage has its own demands and stressors, but each also represents another opportunity to strengthen the homeowner's position and increase pressure on the HOA to settle or comply.

What often surprises homeowners is how many disputes resolve before ever reaching trial. By their mere existence, lawsuits create leverage. The mere fact that a board and its management company (along with its insurance company) know that they will eventually be held accountable in court often helps lead the parties to an eventual settlement. And when boards resist, courts have the authority to order them to follow the law and impose financial consequences for their failures, including paying the homeowner's attorney's fees.

In other words, litigation is not about endless delay and expense for its own sake. It is a structured process that, when handled correctly, can either push an HOA to settle on reasonable terms or force a court to step in and mandate compliance. For homeowners facing entrenched board misconduct, there is no stronger remedy.

When HOA Disputes Escalate Into Litigation

Even when homeowners would rather resolve disputes informally or through pre-litigation ADR, there are times when escalation into litigation becomes unavoidable. These are the situations where the harm is ongoing, the HOA refuses to follow the law, or delay will only make things worse.

Some of the most common triggers include:

- **Architectural denials beyond board authority**. When an HOA blocks improvements despite the protections contained in Civil Code section 4765.

- **Improper fines or due process violations**. When boards impose penalties without following the procedures set out in Civil Code sections 5850–5855.

- **Assessment and collection abuse**. When boards misuse their powers under Civil Code sections 5650–5720, such as imposing illegal assessments or improperly threatening foreclosure.

- **Records stonewalling**. When a board ignores or refuses lawful document inspection requests under Civil Code sections 5200–5235.

- **Election abuse**. When an HOA violates statutory voting requirements under Civil Code sections 5100–5145, undermining the fairness of board elections.

When those types of violations occur, homeowners cannot rely on negotiations alone. If ADR is required, it should be pursued, but when it fails, or when the situation demands stronger remedies, litigation provides the only path to enforce the law. Recognizing these escalation points is critical because waiting too long can entrench board misconduct and make it harder to correct.

How Courts Can Hold HOAs Accountable

When a case ultimately reaches judgment, the court has several tools to hold an HOA accountable. The first is money damages. Courts can order an association to compensate homeowners for the financial harm caused by the board's misconduct. That might mean reimbursing an owner for an illegal fine, paying back improper assessments, compensating a homeowner for the diminution in value of their home, or covering repair costs that the HOA wrongfully refused to make. The nature and scope of the damages available to a homeowner are purely a legal issue, and depend on the causes of action alleged.

In some cases, the Davis-Stirling Act goes beyond a homeowner's monetary damages by authorizing statutory penalties. A good example is when a board refuses to produce records as required under Civil Code sections 5200–5235. In that situation, the law allows homeowners to recover fixed penalties of $500 per request. These penalties are designed to punish the violation and deter future noncompliance, and by framing each separate document demand as a separate demand, the penalties alone equal thousands of dollars.

Courts can also issue what's called injunctive relief. An injunction is an order from the court ordering a party *to do or not do* something. An injunction can force a board to reverse an assessment, provide access to records, correct election procedures, reverse an unlawful architectural denial, or halt collection tactics that don't comply with the law. Unlike damages, injunctions don't just compensate after the fact. They directly change behavior moving forward.

Finally, there is the recovery of attorney's fees and costs. In many HOA disputes (in our experience, most of them), the prevailing party is entitled to recover reasonable attorney's fees and costs. For homeowners, this often turns the financial risk of litigation on its head because a win can mean that the HOA, not the homeowner, will eventually foot the bill for both sides' lawyers. This not only makes lawsuits viable, it creates a strong incentive for boards to respect the law in the first place.

Together, these remedies make litigation the single most powerful enforcement tool available to homeowners. A lawsuit isn't just about winning money. It's about compelling boards to comply with the law, protecting individual rights, and sending a message that abuse of power will not be tolerated.

The Risks of Litigation and How to Manage Them

Litigation, like any serious endeavor, comes with risks. At MBK Chapman, we have a very frank discussion with all of our clients who are considering escalating their cases to litigation. We believe that forewarned is forearmed, and that the more information our clients have, the better prepared they will be to handle the risks. In other words, we work hard to realistically manage our clients' expectations by making sure that they are armed with the information that they need to make wise choices.

The first thing that homeowners should know when they are considering litigation is that if their cases are solid, the risks can be managed with the right preparation and strategy. The point is not to create fear, but to help homeowners make informed decisions and avoid surprises along the way.

The most obvious risk is cost. Lawsuits are not inexpensive, and HOAs know that expense alone can (and does) discourage a lot of members from standing up for their rights. But Davis-Stirling Act's (and many CC&Rs') attorney's fee provisions flip this equation. When homeowners prevail, they can recover their reasonable attorney's fees and costs, often shifting the entire financial burden back onto the HOA. That means the risk of expense is real, but so is the opportunity to neutralize it completely. Of course, even under the best of circumstances, nobody can predict what might happen in court, and if a homeowner loses the case, the homeowner can end up being responsible for the HOA's fees and costs.

Time is another factor. Lawsuits take longer than anyone would like, especially in our post-COVID system. In some California counties, it could take 2-3 years to finally get to trial. That can feel like a burden, but it can also create leverage. Insurance companies aren't in the business of just giving money away, and at some point, they will begin looking closely at the specifics of the case. It is they who will often start applying pressure to their insureds (i.e., the boards) to settle cases. Consequently, with careful case management, time can be turned from an obstacle into an advantage. But typically only after the homeowner's attorney has applied substantial pressure in the form of aggressive litigation.

Make no mistake about it. No litigation outcome is ever guaranteed. Judges and juries have discretion, and cases can take unexpected turns. But this is exactly why working with experienced HOA counsel matters. A strong attorney will identify the weak points early, prepare for the HOA's likely defenses, and build a strategy to maximize the chances of success while minimizing risk.[2]

Another overlooked risk is board retaliation during the pendency of a lawsuit. Some directors may try to use fines, rule enforcement, or social pressure against the homeowner pursuing litigation. Courts take a dim view of retaliation, and in many cases it strengthens the homeowner's claims. But recognizing it early and documenting it thoroughly can turn such bad-faith harassment into an additional lever for accountability.

In short, litigation carries risks. But litigation also carries remedies and rewards that no other process can deliver. When managed correctly, those risks do not outweigh the benefits. They are simply part of the path to holding HOAs accountable and to making homeowners whole.

---

2. That's why it's so important for people to ask very specific questions of their attorneys, including whether the founding partner at the firm has *personally* conducted any trials. If the managing partner of a law firm has no (or little) actual trial experience, how can he or she train or manage the "trial attorneys" below him or her? Ask the question directly, and insist on a clear, written response.

Settlement and Resolution in HOA Lawsuits

As noted at the beginning of this chapter, when a lot of people think of litigation, they picture a dramatic courtroom battle ending with a judge's gavel or a jury verdict. In reality, that's the exception, not the rule. Roughly 95% of civil cases in California settle before trial. HOA disputes are no different.

Settlements happen for many reasons. Litigation is expensive, time-consuming, and stressful for both sides. Boards know that the longer a case drags on, the more money must be pulled from the association's budget or its insurance carrier has to pay legal fees. Insurance companies, in turn, are rarely interested in funding endless battles. At some point, they begin pressuring their insureds, the HOAs, to resolve the cases.

For homeowners, this is not a drawback. It is often the best outcome. A strong settlement can achieve everything a lawsuit was meant to accomplish, such as compliance with the law, reimbursement of illegal fines or assessments, and payment of a homeowner's attorney's fees, all without the uncertainty of a trial. In fact, the possibility of a trial is what drives most settlements. Boards settle because they fear losing in court and facing even greater consequences.

One issue that often arises in settlements is the inclusion of confidentiality or non-disparagement clauses. Boards and their insurers may push for these terms to limit public discussion of the dispute. After all, if your HOA is giving up on a fight with you and/or paying you money, they don't want you telling your fellow homeowners about what you achieved or they could be facing similar lawsuits in the future. While sometimes acceptable (a decision that you'll have to make), homeowners should weigh carefully what they are giving up, especially if the misconduct affected multiple members. An experienced attorney can ensure that any such provisions do not undermine the broader value of the settlement and what's best for you.

It is important to understand that settlement does not mean "giving up." Done correctly, it is both a strategic and real victory. At my firm, when our client has a strong case and the ability, whether perceived or real, to see the case through trial, our strategy is to make it clear to the HOA that settlement will necessarily include full payment of our client's damages and attorney's fees, as well as an agreement that the board will do (or not do) what our client has demanded. In other words, settlement means that our client gets everything he or she is demanding, and that all that will occur is a stop to the bleeding on the HOA's side. That doesn't mean that we don't encourage our clients to agree to a discount on fees if they're getting most everything they've demanded, but it does mean that we always seek to negotiate from a position of strength. Regardless, once a settlement is reached, the result is binding and enforceable, just like a judgment after trial.

In short, while trials make for good television, real-world HOA litigation is usually resolved across the negotiating table. With the right preparation and legal strategy, settlement is not a compromise. It is often the fastest, most efficient way to hold a board accountable and achieve all, or nearly all, of what our clients are seeking.

Got Fined by Your HOA Without Notice? It's Invalid

Despite what people may see in movies or TV shows, your HOA cannot fine you without first holding a formal hearing. In other words, there is no situation where an HOA representative can drive by and issue you a "ticket" and a fine, or where the HOA or management company can send you a letter telling you that you've been fined unless they first held a fully noticed formal hearing and subsequently found you "guilty" of an infraction.

Under California Civil Code section 5855 (as most recently amended by AB 130), your HOA must give you at least 10 days' written notice before holding a disciplinary hearing. That notice has to include the date, time, and reason for the hearing, and it has to provide you with the opportunity to appear and defend yourself.

If they skip that step and go straight to fining you or suspending privileges, the board's action is invalid, and you have every right to demand reversal of the fine.

You can also use their failure as a defense in small claims court or even in a superior court case, especially if the HOA tries to collect on a fine they issued illegally.

This rule protects homeowners from kangaroo-court justice, and it's not optional. If your board thinks it can penalize you in secret, call them on it.

THE HOMEOWNER PLAYBOOK: HOW TO COMBINE RIGHTS TO GAIN LEVERAGE

M OST HOMEOWNERS NEVER think of their rights under the Davis-Stirling Act as a connected system. They demand records when the board hides information, challenge denials of their architectural plans when the board is engaging in selective enforcement, or challenge fines when they feel targeted. But they often see those issues in isolation, one skirmish at a time, without realizing that the law becomes far more powerful when its parts are used together.

Without even consciously realizing it, bad HOA boards thrive on the fact that most homeowners don't know how to connect the dots. Their very existence depends on homeowners treating each dispute as a one-off fight. When you understand that records requests, due process, financial disclosures, dispute resolution, and elections are all pieces of the same puzzle, you stop playing defense and start forcing the board to follow the law across the board.

This chapter shows you how to turn individual rights into a coordinated strategy. You'll see how a single records demand can uncover financial mismanagement that feeds into a disclosure violation, which then becomes leverage in a disciplinary hearing or even a board election challenge. You'll see how mediation or litigation can be the capstone of a layered approach, not the only weapon in your arsenal.

Despite the fact that the Davis-Stirling Act arms HOA boards with sweeping powers that can easily be abused, it does provide the savvy homeowner with the necessary leverage to push back and force compliance with the law. By learning to think strategically, including understanding how to combine the law's protections, you can create accountability in a system designed to favor boards. Done right, this approach shifts you from constantly reacting to abuse to actively steering the outcome.

Turning Individual Rights Into a Coordinated Strategy

Most homeowners approach HOA disputes as one-off battles. They send a letter about a fine, argue over an architectural denial, or complain about an unexplained assessment. Sometimes they get a partial victory, more often they don't. What they rarely do is step back and connect those fights in a way to serve a larger plan. That's the difference between reacting to abuse and forcing accountability.

The key is recognizing that each right afforded to you under the Davis-Stirling Act can be the starting point for another. A records demand under Civil Code section 5200 might reveal that the board hasn't prepared an annual budget summary. That's a violation under sections 5300 and 5310. If the board then tries to impose a special assessment without disclosure, you now have multiple statutory failures that stack together. When you bring that pattern into a disciplinary hearing or ADR, the board is no longer defending a single decision, but rather a record of non-compliance.

Strategic homeowners also know how to use timing. For example, if you know a board election is coming up, requesting financial records before ballots go out can expose mismanagement while members are paying attention (at least more than usual). If you find yourself the victim of selective enforcement, combining a due process challenge with a records demand can uncover whether other owners might have been treated differently. Chances are if you've been targeted with selective enforcement, then others have too.

Keep a simple running list of every issue you spot. Write down the date, what happened, and which right it connects to (i.e., whether it's records, disclosures, due process, or enforcement). Even a basic notebook or spreadsheet will do. Over time, that list can help you spot, transform, and illustrate what was once scattered disputes, into a clear pattern of board misconduct that'll be hard to ignore. If the board still refuses to correct course, you're on your way to building a multi-layered case for mediation or litigation, not just a single gripe.

Thinking this way changes your role. You're not just the member fighting about a landscaping fine. You're the member who demanded records, exposed financial abuse, connected it to missing disclosures, and showed how the board broke due process. That shift makes it harder for the board to dismiss you as a nuisance and easier for a judge, mediator, or even your neighbors to see the board for what it is—non-compliant and unaccountable.

Building Pressure Through Sequencing

Boards can easily ignore a single complaint, but they struggle when homeowners validly assert multiple rights in succession. The order in which you assert your rights matters. A records request that reveals sloppy financials becomes more powerful when followed by a demand for the missing disclosures. A due process challenge carries more weight when paired with evidence that fines weren't adopted under a published fine schedule. An election objection lands harder if it's backed by proof that the board hid reserves or mishandled assessments in the months leading up to the vote.

Think of sequencing as building pressure. Each step gives you leverage for the next. Alone, the steps can be more easily brushed aside. Linked together, they create a chain of accountability that boards can't nearly as easily escape. You also want to be sure to pace your steps. Sequence your requests so that each one sets up the next. In other words, you might make a targeted records demand, wait for the response (or non-response), and *then* follow with the disclosure challenge that the production (or silence) made possible. This cadence creates rolling points of default and avoids giving the board an excuse to claim it was "addressing everything at once."

From Records to Financial Disclosures: Building Leverage

Most homeowners don't file a records request because they care about the HOA's paperwork. They do it because they're fighting something personal, such as a fine, a special assessment, or a denial of their architectural plans. This is where sequencing matters.

When you demand records under Civil Code section 5200, you often uncover holes in the disclosures the HOA is required to give members under sections 5300 and 5310. Those holes may not seem connected to your dispute at first glance, but they give you leverage. For example, if you're challenging a fine, finding that the HOA never adopted a legally required budget or skipped a reserve study lets you argue that the board can't be trusted to enforce discipline when it doesn't even follow its own disclosure laws. If you're seeking a variance for, say, approval for a patio cover or exterior modification, discovering disclosure violations or numerous examples of selective enforcement can pressure the board to back down rather than risk a paper trail showing multiple statutory failures.

The point isn't to fix the HOA's reporting. The point is to build pressure. Boards know that disclosure violations can lead to statutory penalties and personal liability for directors. When you connect a records demand to missing disclosures, you're no longer just one homeowner arguing over a fine or a variance. You're the homeowner who can prove the board broke state law. That pressure often makes boards more willing to compromise and grant the relief you're actually after.

A records request under Civil Code section 5200 et seq. isn't just about reviewing meeting minutes or bank ledgers. When you compare what the board produces against the disclosures it must provide under sections 5300 and 5310 (which we discussed at length in Chapter 5), inconsistencies often emerge. Maybe the budget summary doesn't match the reserve account statements. Maybe the board distributed a reserve study "summary" but never actually commissioned the full study that the law requires. Maybe the percent funded number doesn't track when looking at the full reserve study from which it came. Or maybe the insurance information disclosed to members is out of date or missing entirely.

That's why it helps to look not just at the finished disclosures, but at the underlying materials behind them. Ask for the reserve study's full component list, the assumptions used by the preparer, any engagement letters, and the board minutes or resolutions adopting budgets or fine schedules. Comparing those inputs to what was disclosed often reveals the gap between what the board reported publicly and what it actually relied upon internally.

Those kinds of gaps are more than sloppy administration. And once you can document them, the conversation changes. You're no longer arguing about whether the board should be more transparent. You're showing that the board has failed to meet mandatory obligations required by the Davis-Stirling Act. That proof not only gives you substantial leverage in the moment, but it also lays the foundation for your next move, whether it's "convincing" the board to go ahead and provide you with the variance that you're seeking, demanding corrective disclosures, raising the issue at a disciplinary hearing, or using it in mediation to get the mediator arguing your side to the HOA.

The sequencing is what matters. A single records request might get brushed off. But when you immediately link what you find (or don't find) to the board's disclosure duties, you force the board into a position where each failure amplifies the next. *That kind of layered accountability is what turns individual rights into real power.*

Due Process: Using Hearing Abuses as Ammunition

When boards mishandle disciplinary hearings, they hand homeowners who are in the know leverage. Civil Code section 5855 requires them to give you notice, allows you to present your side, and to issue a written decision. If they skip any of those steps, the fine is vulnerable, no matter what the board claims you did wrong, and no matter how "guilty" you may be.

That leverage goes beyond getting a single fine reversed. If you're fighting a variance denial, proof that the board routinely ignores due process strengthens your case if ADR ever becomes necessary. If the board tries to collect fines through small claims, you can point to those violations as a legal defense to demonstrate a pattern and practice of abuse by the board. And if you head to court, a judge is far more likely to side with you when you can show the board didn't follow its own statutory obligations.

The point isn't to win an abstract argument. The point is to turn the board's sloppiness into ammunition that protects your pocketbook and forces better outcomes. We've used due process violations to stop lien threats, to get thousands of dollars in fines refunded, and to pressure boards into granting approvals they otherwise would have fought.

Selective Enforcement: Turning Abuse Into a Legal Weapon

Selective enforcement occurs when a board applies HOA rules or standards inconsistently. It can take the form of uneven discipline, e.g., fining one homeowner for a violation while ignoring the same condition at another property, but it also shows up in architectural control, where one homeowner's plans are denied while another homeowner's nearly identical plans are approved. In fact, selective enforcement can happen with rule enforcement, architectural decisions, amenity privileges, or even access to association resources. What makes it "selective" is not the rule itself, but the way the board chooses to enforce it.

California law does not allow HOAs to apply restrictions arbitrarily or in a way that singles out some members while favoring others. When you can document selective enforcement, you gain a powerful defense against penalties, denials, or restrictions, and a legal weapon that shifts leverage back to you.

Boards rely on selective enforcement because it keeps homeowners off balance. They punish one person for a patio cover while ignoring the exact same structure in three backyards down the street. They reject your garage conversion while quietly approving your neighbor's. They fine you for leaving trash cans out overnight while letting their allies slide. On the surface, these examples look like board politics or personal grudges. In reality, they're legal vulnerabilities that you can absolutely use to your advantage.

The sequencing matters. If you're fined or denied a variance, don't stop with your own dispute. Document similar violations throughout the community. Photograph the pergola two doors down, the landscaping across the street, the garage door down the block. Tie those examples directly to your case. In IDR or ADR, you can frame the board's decision as selective enforcement and push for dismissal. If the HOA forces the issue into court, you can use those records as evidence to shift the risk back onto the board.

This strategy doesn't just protect you from fines or demolitions. It creates leverage. Sometimes, really powerful leverage. A board that enforces selectively risks losing in court and paying your attorney's fees. Faced with that exposure, boards often grant the approval or drop the penalty rather than gambling on defending their double standards. For homeowners, that's the path from being singled out to turning the HOA's own behavior into a weapon.

Case Study

A client of mine built a permanent greenhouse in the backyard without HOA approval. It wasn't a small garden shed. It was a $75,000 structure, built on a cement foundation, wired with electricity, and positioned squarely in the setback. On paper, the HOA had every advantage. Let me be clear. My client absolutely violated both the

CC&Rs and the Architectural Guidelines when he built the greenhouse. Not only did he build it within a prohibited setback, but he built it without seeking prior HOA approval. The HOA's attorney sent a formal demand threatening litigation if my client didn't tear down and remove the greenhouse.

My client did not want to tear it down. He had invested heavily, and the greenhouse was built to last. *More importantly, we knew that the only reason it was an issue was because the President of the HOA did not like my client.*

So instead of conceding, I built leverage. I flew a drone over the community and documented how dozens of other properties, including those of board members, had pergolas, sheds, play structures, and BBQs inside their setbacks. Some were even more obvious violations than my client's greenhouse, yet the board had apparently ignored all of them. This was not a modest neighborhood. These were multimillion-dollar homes. Enforcing the rules consistently would have required demolishing backyard improvements worth millions more in aggregate.

In my demand letter, I forced the board to face that reality. In addition to presenting 11 pages of pictures demonstrating dozens of other properties with violating structures, I also called out the hypocrisy driving the dispute. I wrote:

> "The HOA President herself maintains unapproved structures within her setback, yet she is leading the charge to force my client to remove

his greenhouse. This is selective enforcement at its most blatant."

At that point, the HOA had no good options. If they chose litigation, they risked losing on selective enforcement grounds and being ordered to pay my client's attorney's fees. If they enforced consistently, they would have enraged the entire community.

The board folded. The settlement let my client keep the greenhouse. In return, my client granted a concession to plant two or three small trees along the property line to block the greenhouse's limited street visibility. My client kept a $75,000 structure that should have been demolished had the rules been evenly enforced. What looked like a hopeless violation became an unqualified win because I turned the HOA's own hypocrisy into leverage.

From Mediation to Litigation: Forcing a Board Into the Open

Mediation following a formal ADR demand doesn't always end with a handshake and a settlement agreement. While we resolve over 50% of our pre-litigation cases at mediation (without ever having to file a lawsuit), that leaves a good number of cases that haven't settled. Sometimes the board refuses to participate at all. Other times, it shows up but stonewalls or takes an absurd position that is contrary to the law.

That may feel like a dead end, but in practice, it's an opportunity. A failed mediation will never weaken your case.[1]

If the board refuses to mediate following your ADR demand and it somehow wins at trial, Civil Code section 5960 allows a court to consider that refusal when deciding how much to award in attorney's fees. Judges don't look kindly on HOAs that ignore their statutory duty to sit down with their own members. If the board wastes that opportunity, you can point to it later as proof that it litigated in bad faith. That's often enough to shift the financial risk of a lawsuit squarely onto the association.

Even when mediation happens but the dispute doesn't settle, you still walk away with leverage. When the board spends thousands of dollars on lawyers to fight instead of settling a straightforward dispute, other homeowners start to notice. They wonder why their dues are funding conflict instead of maintenance. That kind of exposure is a form of accountability. Boards that thrive on secrecy hate being forced into the open, and sometimes the best leverage you gain from ADR is that the HOA's refusal becomes a story you can use to inform your neighbors.

While neither side is allowed to publicize anything filed in mediation (California law makes that process strictly confidential), everything filed in court is public record. Once your case reaches litigation, you can circulate the board's pleadings, as well as your own, to all of the other homeowners. Nothing educates the community faster than showing them, in the board's own words, what it's spending money to fight about. When neighbors see the HOA (or its insurance company) pouring resources into opposing a legitimate homeowner's reasonable request, it stops being just your battle and starts being theirs too.

In short, mediation is not a dead end even if the case fails to settle. It's a spotlight. If the board uses it to act reasonably, you can reach resolution. If it refuses or stonewalls, you can turn that refusal into

---

1. For example, since we always keep our mediation briefs strictly confidential (meaning that only the mediators ever see them), there is no risk of our ever educating the HOAs as to our case strategies.

ammunition—financially, legally, and politically. Either way, you move forward stronger than you were before.

Stacking Your Rights to Apply Maximum Pressure

Up to this point, we've looked at how to build pressure by sequencing your rights, starting with records, tying them to disclosures, using due process failures as ammunition, exposing selective enforcement, and forcing boards into the open. The next step is learning how to combine those moves into full strategies. Think of these not as isolated plays, but as playbook combinations that, when used together, force the board to make concessions it would never have made if you only pressed on one front.

That doesn't mean you need a master plan on day one. Most homeowners don't. Stacking happens naturally as a dispute unfolds. But if you don't know where to look, you'll never see it. You make a records demand and discover disclosure violations. You face a fine and realize the board skipped due process. You seek a variance and uncover selective enforcement. Each step gives you another right to add to the pile, until the board isn't facing a single fight, but rather a coordinated attack it can't win.

The Variance Play

Few fights matter more to homeowners than architectural approvals. Whether it's a greenhouse, a patio cover, a garage conversion, or new landscaping, these projects involve real money and real property value. When the board denies an application, most owners think they're stuck. But that's where stacking comes in.

Start with selective enforcement. If your board approved a neighbor's pergola, shed, or garage conversion but denied yours, you already have your first pressure point. Document those comparisons. Then add records. Demand architectural committee minutes and records showing what approvals the board has granted in the past. If those records don't exist, or if they expose inconsistent treatment, you've created a second pressure point. Finally, add process. If the board denied your application without giving you a chance to present your plans in a fair hearing, or if the board fails to properly explain the basis for its denial, that due process violation becomes a third pressure point.

Individually, each of those flaws might not be enough to move the board (although they should). Together, they box the board in. Approve your variance, and the problem goes away. Deny it, and the board faces a selective enforcement claim, a records violation, and a due process failure all at once, plus the risk of paying your attorney's fees if you litigate. That's the power of stacking. What began as a single denial turns into a campaign the board can't afford to fight.

The Recall Play

Most HOA members tune out board elections. Turnout is low, apathy is high, and incumbents coast back into power. But recalls are different. When directors abuse their authority, hide financial mismanagement, or target members unfairly, nothing gets the community's attention faster than the chance to throw them out mid-term. Stacking your rights makes that recall effort stronger.

Start with disclosures. If the board failed to deliver a reserve study or budget summary, or if it pushed through assessments without the required notices or votes, those violations aren't just technicalities. They're ammunition. Homeowners who never attend meetings start paying attention when they learn that their dues are rising or a special assessment is looming on the horizon while the board ignores basic financial reporting.

Add records. Demand financials and membership lists. Financials let you show your neighbors exactly what's been hidden, while the membership list gives you the ability to send details to your fellow members, as well as to campaign for signatures and circulate recall petitions without relying on board-controlled communication.

Regarding the membership list in particular, make sure that you tell the board that you intend to use it solely for association-related communications. Then, when you reach out to your fellow homeowners, be sure to keep your communications factual and sourced (cite produced records, minutes, and disclosures). Staying within those bounds preserves your credibility and avoids giving the board a pretext to attack the recall effort instead of answering for its conduct. If the board resists, that stonewalling itself becomes part of your message. Directors are hiding information and violating the Davis-Stirling Act because they know their positions won't survive scrutiny.

Finally, layer in selective enforcement or due process abuses. If directors are fining certain members while excusing their allies, or if they denied you or your neighbors a fair hearing, you have concrete examples of favoritism and lawlessness. If the board is doing it to you, then they're doing it to other homeowners. Get the word out. Nothing galvanizes support for a recall faster than showing how those in power use rules as weapons against people that they don't like.

One issue alone might not rally the community. But stacked together—financial violations, secrecy, and abusive enforcement—you create a recall campaign that fellow homeowners can rally around. At that point, it's no longer about legal technicalities. It's about money, fairness, and survival in the community. That's when neighbors sign, vote, and remove bad boards.

The Financial Pressure Play

Nothing gets homeowners' attention faster than money. When a board announces a steep dues increase or slaps the community with a sudden special assessment, members want to know why. Stacking your rights lets you turn that outrage into leverage.

Start with records. Demand the financials and reserve studies. If the board skipped a required reserve study under Civil Code section 5550, or failed to distribute the annual budget disclosures under section 5300, you've already identified statutory violations.

As you saw in Chapter 9, reserve studies and annual disclosures are not just paperwork. They are statutory leverage points. When boards ignore them, they hand you evidence of financial mismanagement that can be stacked with other violations to increase your leverage.

Add disclosures. Missing or misleading annual disclosures show that the board tried to hide the problem. Even worse, some boards manipulate reserve studies by, for example, defunding certain assets or removing them entirely, to artificially inflate the "percent funded" number and make the HOA's financial position look stronger than it really is. That kind of manipulation lets directors claim the community is well-funded while quietly setting up members for sudden, crushing special assessments down the line. When you uncover it, you don't just show negligence, you expose deliberate misrepresentation.

Stacked together, this becomes more than a debate about numbers. It's a campaign that shows the board broke the law, hid information, and wasted money. Homeowners see the assessment as the final straw, and you gain the leverage to push for reductions, extended payment plans, or even reimbursement. The board can fight, but each move digs it in deeper, raising both its legal exposure and its political risk.

The Accountability Play

Sometimes stacking your rights doesn't end with settlement. Sometimes the board refuses to compromise, and the dispute heads to court. That might sound daunting, but even litigation gives you leverage because once a case is filed, the fight is no longer hidden. It becomes part of the public record.

By statute, mediation is confidential. Neither side can use what was said there as a weapon outside the room. Court is different. But as I pointed out earlier in this chapter, every pleading, motion, and declaration the HOA (or you) files becomes part of the public record. And that record belongs not just to you, but to every member of the community. When they see the association spending dues money (or wasting insurance) to fight a homeowner over a patio cover, a parking space, or a disclosure violation, the politics of the HOA can change overnight.

You can also use the lawsuit itself as a spotlight. If the board ignored your records demand, skipped due process, or manipulated the reserve study, those failures are now front and center before a judge. By the time you're in court, you aren't just asking for relief, you're showing a documented pattern of abuse. That pattern, now public, forces the board to defend its behavior to more than just a judge. It has to defend it to the people footing the bill, i.e., your fellow HOA members.

The risk to the HOA multiplies. If it loses, it will have to pay your attorney's fees on top of its own. And all the while, its pleadings are circulating in the community, undermining whatever political capital the directors thought they had left. Boards that thrive on secrecy hate litigation for exactly this reason.

That's the ultimate value of stacking. You don't just fight on one front. You build layer after layer of pressure until the board faces a no-win choice to settle, concede, or watch the fight play out in public.

CONCLUSION

I F YOU'VE MADE it this far, you now see the full picture. HOAs are given enormous power under the Davis-Stirling Act, and HOAs from Hell use that power to abuse the rights of homeowners. They impose fines without due process, selectively enforce rules, deny improvements arbitrarily, hide financials, manipulate reserve studies, run elections to entrench themselves, and stonewall members who ask questions. The law is lopsided. The deck is stacked against you.

But you've also seen something else. The law does not render you powerless. The Davis-Stirling Act may give boards the upper hand, but it also gives homeowners a series of powerful rights that can be turned into pressure points. Records demands. Disclosure rights. Due process guarantees. Restrictions on selective enforcement. Dispute resolution procedures. Voting and recall rights. Each of these on its own may not feel like enough. But when you use them together, they become leverage the board cannot ignore.

That's the real message of this book. You cannot wait for a bad HOA to "do the right thing." You have to force compliance.

And you can.

Homeowners who understand how to demand records, call out disclosure failures, challenge fines, expose selective enforcement, and, when needed, drag boards into mediation or even court, shift the balance of power. Stacking your rights turns isolated disputes into campaigns that bad boards simply can't win.

You also know by now that this isn't theory. We've shown how these strategies work in real disputes. A greenhouse variance kept in place, fines wiped out because the board never adopted a schedule, selective enforcement turned into a weapon, financial mismanagement exposed. The system may be unfair, but it's not unbeatable.

So what do you do next?

You act.

Don't sit back and hope things improve. Use this playbook. Demand records. Review the disclosures. Document selective enforcement. Take pictures. Take videos. Talk to your neighbors. Circulate recall petitions when necessary.

And when the board still refuses to follow the law, demand IDR, take them into ADR, or file a lawsuit. You can do these things because you now have the tools to fight back and win.

This book is called HOA HELL because that's what it feels like to live under an abusive board.

But it's also a map out of it.

With the strategies here, you're not just surviving. You're fighting back, using the very law the board thought it could hide behind. And you can continue to gain strategies, tips, and tricks by listening to my podcast, HOA HELL. You'll find the podcast on YouTube, Amazon, Apple, Spotify, and other platforms.

You don't have to accept abuse. You don't have to let directors waste your money or trample your rights. You don't have to stay powerless. You can demand compliance. You can organize. You can litigate. And you can win.

That's your way out of HOA Hell.

Acknowledgements

I want to thank my son, Logan, whose encouragement and curiosity continue to inspire my work.

Special thanks go to associate attorney at MBK Chapman, Torri Patel, Esq., whose own path as a writer has been a constant source of motivation.

Special thanks also goes to a senior associate at MBK Chapman, Sam Khil, co-host of the HOA HELL podcast, and trusted proofreader whose insights strengthened this book.

Finally, I am grateful to the dedicated attorneys and staff of MBK Chapman, whose daily commitment to our mission makes everything possible.

About the Author

Michael Kushner is a lifelong resident of Southern California and one of the foremost authorities on homeowner-side HOA law in California. For almost 30 years, he has represented homeowners (not HOA boards) in some of the most hard-fought HOA disputes in the state. Widely regarded as the homeowner-side pioneer in this field, he built the pre-litigation systems and strategies that the two largest homeowner-side law firms in California still use today.

Michael earned his undergraduate degree at UC Berkeley and his law degree at UCLA. Over the course of his nearly 30-year career, his firm has counseled thousands of clients throughout the State of California regarding all manner of HOA-related disputes and litigation. He has also authored numerous articles on HOA law from the homeowner's perspective, lectured widely on business and HOA litigation strategies, and established himself as a trusted voice for Californians battling abusive associations.

Outside the courtroom, Michael is the host of the popular podcast HOA HELL, where he translates complex HOA disputes into clear strategies that homeowners can use to fight back. His work through the show has expanded his reach far beyond his law firm, giving thousands of homeowners across the state tools to understand and enforce their rights.

Beyond the law, Michael is a third-degree black belt in Kenpo Karate and an avid woodworker. On any given day, when he's not working, Michael can be found either in his woodshop where he builds custom chessboards, charcuterie and cheese boards, and fine tea boxes, or teaching karate to others. His greatest pride, however, is his son Logan, who will soon be starting law school and plans to join MBK Chapman to continue the mission of holding California HOAs accountable.